CLICK

The Art + Science of Getting from Impasse to Insight

Eve Grodnitzky, PhD

CLICK: The Art + Science of Getting from Impasse to Insight
Copyright © 2014 Eve Grodnitzky

Published by:
Blooming Twig Books
New York / Tulsa
www.bloomingtwig.com

Cover design by Heather Neil
Treasure map and chapter page illustrations by Lauren Scott
Archimedes illustration by Andre Thevet (1564), Wikimedia Commons
Bloodhound photograph by PlePle2000, Wikimedia Commons
Stereogram & Shark by Fredshu, Wikimedia Commons
All other photographs courtesy of author

Hardcover: ISBN 978-1-61343-064-4
Softcover: ISBN 978-1-61343-065-1
eBook: ISBN 978-1-61343-066-8

United States — First Edition

Printed in the United States of America.

To Gustavo,
for everything that is wonderful and human.

And to Merlin and Bella,
for everything that is wonderful and canine.

Table of Contents

PREFACE

In February of 2011, standing alone on a snowy mountain in Canada and feeling fairly sure that I was about to die in one of several extremely unpleasant ways, I had the moment of insight that set me on the path towards writing this book.

Gustavo (my now-husband / then-boyfriend) and I were on a ski vacation at Whistler, a couple of hours outside of Vancouver in British Columbia. Gustavo is an expert skier – and I, being a good sport and a savvy girlfriend, was trying to become…a less pathetic skier. By the time of our trip to Whistler, I was generally able to make it down the easiest runs (the "green runs" – so designated by the solid green circles on the signs that mark the beginner trails) – but more through sheer force of will and "muscling it" rather than through any sort of skill or technique. And most of the time – I'm not gonna lie – I was terrified. But the man I loved loved skiing, so darn it, I was gonna get the hang of this. Even if it killed me, which I was starting to think it just might.

It was the final day of our trip to Whistler, and Gustavo and I were skiing a green run together down from the top of the mountain, having taken the mid-mountain lift up to the top just as they were shutting it down. About halfway back down the mountain, a black diamond (i.e., expert) run broke off to the left, and I encouraged Gustavo to go have fun on that trail while I finished off this little green run on my own. According to our trail maps, the two trails rejoined at a lift a little farther down the mountain, so we could just meet up there and ski an easy green run down the rest of the mountain together. After multiple reassurances that yes, I'd be just fine doing the rest of this green run myself, Gustavo gave me a big smile, poled over the edge and was on his way down the expert slope.

With Gustavo on his way, I took another look at my trail map, just to make sure I knew how to get to our agreed-upon rendezvous point, then stuffed the map back in my pocket, put on my gloves and began to (somewhat inelegantly, I'm sure) make my way down the run. Several minutes later I arrived at the mid-mountain lift…only to find that Gustavo wasn't there. The lift itself was already shut down, so in fact there wasn't anyone there at all. I skied over to the big trail map to make sure I was at the right place…and I was. There just wasn't any Gustavo.

The most troubling of the various thoughts that began to run through my head was the concern that he'd had an accident of some kind. I pulled out my cell phone and called him. No answer. I texted him. No response. I waited for another ten minutes, and there still wasn't any sign of him. In fact, there wasn't any sign of anyone, since the mountain was closing down for the day and it was beginning to snow. Hard.

Out of options, I decided that I'd have to ski the rest of the way down on my own and hope that he'd be at the bottom of the mountain waiting for me (along with a really good explanation). Skiing down the mountain all alone, as the light was fading and the snow was beginning to come down in earnest, I actually had a brief moment where I understood why people really love skiing. Having Whistler Mountain all to myself in the snow and the silence was really quite magical.

Part of the way down the mountain, I stopped and pulled out my camera and took a little video in an attempt to capture the beauty and the peacefulness of the experience. Putting my camera back into my pocket, I continued to ski down the rest of the run and across an open, meadow-like area that I expected would connect me to the next green run that I'd planned to take the rest of the way down the mountain.

Skiing up to the break in the trees that indicated the start of that next run, I looked up at the sign indicating the name of the run: "Crabapple." Buuuuut…wait a minute here. That's not the run I was expecting. And it's got a blue square next to it, rather than a green circle. That means it's an intermediate run, not a beginner run. That can't be. This is supposed to be a green run. I planned it all on the map that I just looked at by the lift a few minutes ago higher up the mountain.

Well, crap. Somehow, in my desire to capture the beauty of the setting on camera, I must have gotten a bit disoriented and taken a wrong turn somewhere. But no worries, I'll just pull out my trail map and find the green run I was looking for – it's got to be around here somewhere.

So out comes the trail map…and I realize that the green run I'd intended to take is in the opposite corner of the meadow I've just crossed. And it's easily several hundred yards away. Uphill.

Houston, we have a problem.

It's freezing cold, night is beginning to fall, I'm alone, it's now snowing heavily…and I'm screwed. I'm standing at the top of a ski run that I *cannot* do – looking at a distant run that I *can* do, but that I can't get to.

For several minutes I stand there, frozen in place, looking over the edge of Crabapple (i.e., The Cliff of Death) – and then looking up the full length of the meadow at the far-away entrance to the green run. Time is running out in a very serious way. It's genuinely starting to get dark now, which is going to force me to make a decision. I am terrified. Utterly petrified with fear. I consider it a real possibility that I could die in a spectacular and horrific crash if I try to make it down Crabapple. But trying to make it uphill to the distant green run isn't practical in these conditions; they would find my frozen body lying in the snow halfway across the meadow the next morning.

Crap.

I stand there, immobilized by fear and indecision for another minute, my mind racing. It might not be a near-death experience by conventional standards, but in that moment, it sure feels like it.

Then, seemingly out of nowhere, a simple question appears in my mind: "Meh, how hard could it be?"

Suddenly, everything just clicks into place. It's as if the world has tilted on its axis. The tension in my body vanishes. Fear transforms into acceptance, and my mind is quiet. The decision is made: Crabapple it is. I even have the wherewithal to pull out my camera and take a self-portrait with the Crabapple sign behind me as proof of my choice. Then I put the camera away, grab my poles, take a deep breath – and push myself over the edge of the cliff. I'm off.

Moments before starting down Crabapple.

Preface

And it's spectacular. It's taking every ounce of strength and concentration I have, but I'm doing it. I'm sure it isn't pretty to look at – and it's taking everything I have – but I'm doing it.

A few minutes later, I schuss my way into the meeting zone at the bottom of the mountain – and find a very concerned-looking Gustavo. He'd taken a wrong turn too, and only realized it long after there was any way to get back to our original rendezvous point. So he'd done the same thing that I'd done – decided to ski to the bottom in the hope that we'd find each other there, safe and sound. And he'd been anxiously waiting there, scanning the mountain, for what seemed like ages.

I tell him of my blue run triumph, and we share a congratulatory embrace and start back towards the lodge. Victory is mine – and so is the start of an incredible personal and professional journey, though I don't realize it just yet (I'm too busy enjoying the fact that I'm still alive and unbroken).

In the days and weeks following The Crabapple Incident, I thought a lot about that transformative experience on the mountain and the moment when some little voice inside my head posed that fateful question: "Meh, how hard could it be?" They were only six words, but they empowered me to do something that – literally the *instant* before – I was 100% convinced that I could not do. Suddenly, everything just…clicked.

The more I thought about what happened that afternoon on the ski slope, the more I started to realize the tremendous power of my seemingly innocuous little question. To the extent that I could translate that attitude to other things in my life, what else might be possible? I'd already done some pretty bold things in my life – gotten a Ph.D., started my own business, jumped out of several perfectly good airplanes, and galloped a horse among giraffe and rhinoceros in Africa. But how many other things – both personal and professional – might I have been missing out on because I was "100% convinced" that I couldn't do them? What if the truth was that it wasn't the *actual* difficulty of the things themselves that prevented me from doing them – it was my *perception* of their difficulty?

As I became fully aware of the life-changing power of that moment of insight, I started to reflect in a more deliberate way on other insight experiences that had happened previously in my life – and how profoundly they had impacted me and influenced the major decisions that I'd made. I didn't always realize it at the time, but with the benefit of hindsight, I came to recognize that most of my life's major turning points – both personal and professional – were set in motion by an insight experience of one type or another. And now that I was actively focused on infusing my life with the (quite unexpected) power of these insights, I also started to wonder if there was a way that I could share what I had learned with other people so that they could leverage the power of insights too.

It was this desire – to help both individuals and organizations increase the frequency of insights and fully harness their transformative power – that led me to research and write this book. As you read the following chapters, I hope that the insight-generation approach I've outlined both enables and inspires you to have more insights of your own – and put them to work for you as well.

INTRODUCTION

If you ask my parents, I've always been a teacher. My mom tells a story about coming to pick me up at preschool or kindergarten one day and finding me sitting on the curb next to a bunch of other little kids in my class, trying to teach them how to tie their shoes. Apparently I had already mastered that skill (this was in the days before Velcro®, so shoe-tying was quite the critical life skill), and now I was trying to teach all the other kids how to do it too. In the spirit of full disclosure, my mom says that I did get a bit frustrated when some of the other kids weren't so quick on the uptake, but at least my heart was in the right place.

Fast-forward a couple of decades to graduate school at the University of Michigan, where I was pursuing my Ph.D. in Social Psychology. Like pretty much every other student in the history of grad school, I ended up having to be a T.A. (teaching assistant) to help pay my way through school – and I really did *not* think I would enjoy it. But, much to my surprise, I actually loved it. I even loved office hours, which most of my colleagues hated. Personally, there was nothing more satisfying for me as a T.A. than helping someone "get it"; helping them work through something they were confused about until everything just suddenly clicked into place and they exclaimed, "Oh my gosh! I totally understand now!"

Another few years down the line and I was working for a well-respected research and consulting firm, teaching senior executives at Fortune 500 companies and major government organizations. Everything from leadership development to performance management to employee engagement to attraction and retention of high-performing employees. Try teaching structural equation modeling to a room full of HR professionals, and you'll know what a good time is.

A few years later and I was splitting my time between running my own leadership development and public-speaking company and doing a bunch of contract work for that same research and consulting firm, plus another large executive education organization.

I was doing lots of good work with interesting research, great colleagues and some really cool organizations....but...I began to wonder how much of a difference I was really making in people's lives. As hard as I was working, I couldn't shake the sense that, somehow, there was more I could be doing to help make the world a better place, as corny as that sounds.

So I started to think about what additional things might be possible. What did I feel intensely passionate about? What could I do that would make even more of a difference for people and for organizations? If I could teach anything – anything at all – what would it be?

I kept coming back to the various pearls of wisdom that my moments of insight have given me over the course of my life. Those are the things that have most significantly helped me improve my own life, and I started to wonder if there was some way that I could share them and their power with other folks. As I continued to think about possibilities, it occurred to me that perhaps the real power wouldn't come from sharing my own insights with other people – because what's revelatory for me might not be revelatory for someone else. There are really useful lessons that my insights have taught me that other people could probably benefit from as well, but the real power of those insights came from the fact that I had them *myself*. As a result, they were both intensely personal – and empowering. And so I started to think that my focus shouldn't be teaching other people about my insights – maybe it should be teaching people how to unleash *their own* insights.

Introduction

If I could identify a process that could help people achieve their own breakthrough moments – both personally and professionally – now *that* would be a worthy calling. But is that even possible? In our day-to-day lives, insight experiences seem to arrive (or not) on their own terms – and usually when we least expect them. Is there actually a way to facilitate a process that seems so incredibly elusive?

Yes, as it turns out, there is. The book that you're holding in your hands now is the culmination of a research process that was uniquely challenging – in large part because the general consensus of academic researchers who work in this area is that we really don't know how insight works. We're fascinated by insight – and various studies are chipping away at it here and there – but efforts to capture it in the lab have largely been like trying to grab smoke with your hands. Insight can be maddeningly elusive.

It is also important to note that although research in related areas such as problem-solving, creativity and innovation can help supplement our understanding of insight, insight itself is a distinct phenomenon with characteristics and mechanisms that are unique to it. Thanks to lots of great research over many decades, researchers have a reasonably good handle on how problem-solving, creativity and innovation work. Insight? Not so much.

Where science does have answers to parts of the insight question, I'll share those and talk about how they influenced the development of what I call my Impasse to Insight Method. That said, the full richness of the Method doesn't derive exclusively from science's currently limited understanding of the mechanisms of insight – it also derives from deep, qualitative analysis of the insight experiences of real people that I'll share throughout this book (including my own) – plus hundreds of others that I encountered in my research. Looking across the richness of these experiences, certain patterns become apparent – and it's those patterns that form the foundation of the Impasse to Insight Method.

The chapters of this book represent the critical steps in the insight-generation process as I've come to understand them. I begin with a look at the history of insight and offer a framework for thinking about the different types of insight that we can experience. From there, I outline, step-by-step, the process by which insight generally unfolds – and how you can actively accelerate the insight-generation process. While I won't go so far as to suggest that following the Impasse to Insight Method will guarantee that you can produce insights "on demand," it will certainly give you the understanding and tools you need to facilitate the process.

I tend to think about it in terms of the following analogy. Unless you're Iceman of Marvel Comics X-Men fame, you can't "force" water to turn into ice on demand using your superhero powers. Nor can you point a gun at a glass of water and say, "Freeze – or the bottled water gets it!" However, you *can create conditions* where freezing is highly likely (i.e., drop the temperature below 32 degrees Fahrenheit and let nature take its course). It's much the same with insight. You can't "force" insight to appear on demand – but you *can create conditions* where it's highly likely to occur. This book provides an understanding of what those conditions are and how you can put them to use for you.

To help make this book as user-friendly as possible, each chapter includes two versions of a summary of the key points in that chapter. The "In a Nutshell" section towards the beginning of each chapter gives you a brief overview of the critical concepts that you'll learn in that chapter. And to make it even easier for you to put into practice what you learn, each chapter ends with a section called "So What?" These "So What?" sections summarize the key learning points of each chapter and offer specific, tactical implementation guidance for the practices presented in that chapter. Consider them the quick-and-dirty how-to guides for insight generation.

I know the tremendous power that insights have to transform lives for the better because I've experienced this power myself and because I've spoken with countless people who have generously shared their own insight stories with me in the course of researching this book. What's been particularly exciting for me to discover is that, although each experience of insight is unique, there are common threads that weave

Introduction

through all of them that provide a methodology for facilitating insight generation. I hope that this book provides you with both the knowledge and the inspiration to create the conditions for more insights in your own life. If it does, please reach out and share your stories with me, as I'd love to hear them!

Eve Grodnitzky, November 2013
insights@evegrodnitzky.com

CLICK

**The Art + Science of Getting
from Impasse to Insight**

CHAPTER 1

From Archimedes to the Anterior Cingulate Cortex:
A Brief History of Insight

Nothing says "moment of insight" quite like an old man running naked through the streets of ancient Greece while shouting, "Eureka!"

The story of Archimedes and the purity of the king's crown is arguably the oldest – and certainly the most iconic – of history's moments of insight that are recorded in Western literature. Born in the ancient Greek colony of Syracuse on the island of Sicily (now part of Italy) in 287 B.C., Archimedes was a mathematician, inventor, scientist, and philosopher – a Renaissance Man a good 1600 years before the actual Renaissance. With regard to his famous streaking incident, the story goes something like this. A crown was made for a Greek king, but there was some question as to whether the crown was pure gold or whether the goldsmith had mixed in a bit of (cheaper) silver as well. Alas, since the crown was already completed, no one could think of a way to determine whether it was pure gold or a cheap knock-off. Eventually, it fell to Archimedes (who was generally considered one of the smartest guys around) to resolve the issue. Unfortunately, after working tirelessly on the issue for some time, he was no closer to a solution.

Frustrated, Archimedes headed for the public baths and a stress-reducing soak. As he was lowering himself into the bath, he happened to notice the water rising up and splashing over the side of the tub. *The more of Archimedes there was in the bathtub...the less water there was in the bathtub.* And, just like that, Archimedes suddenly had his solution to the purity-of-the-crown problem. He could measure the *volume* of the crown by putting it in a container of water and measuring the volume of water that the crown displaced. For the sake of argument, let's say the crown displaced one cup of water. He could then weigh the crown against that same volume (one cup) of pure gold. If the scales balanced, the crown was pure gold. If the scales did *not* balance, the gold had been diluted with some other metal (and, presumably, it was off with the crown-maker's head).

In his excitement, Archimedes is rumored to have leapt from the bath and run naked through the streets shouting, "Eureka!" (translation from the Greek: "I have found it!").

Dramatic license or not, it makes for a memorable story. In addition, it gives us the first recorded moment (at least in Western literature) of genuine insight - also known as a "Eureka moment," an "Aha Moment" and a "Light Bulb Moment." Whatever you call it, it's that moment of blinding clarity when a truth or a solution suddenly springs upon you – seemingly out of nowhere – and everything just clicks into place.

In a Nutshell

One of the challenges of writing a book on insight is finding robust scientific research on the topic. When I began to research the concept of insight in earnest, I was struck by a number of things, one of which was how relatively little work there seems to be in this space, compared to other (frankly less interesting) topics. For a concept that was so totally rocking my world, I was surprised to discover that it wasn't also rocking everyone else's.

What I also noticed was how relatively little agreement there was among the research that did exist. Even experts in the field admitted that what we *don't* know about insight far exceeds what we do know.

From Archimedes to the Anterior Cingulate Cortex

Researchers William H. Batchelder and Gregory E. Alexander, writing in *The Journal of Problem Solving* (2012)[1], lamented, "It is our position that very little is known empirically or theoretically about the cognitive processes involved in solving insight problems. Furthermore, this lack of knowledge stands in stark contrast with other areas of cognition such as human memory, decision-making, categorization, and perception."

If misery loves company, there's a lot of company among insight researchers, who continue to be intrigued and frustrated by insight in equal measure. Fortunately, although research can't yet tell us everything about insight, it can at least begin to illuminate a path towards greater understanding. In this chapter I provide a (relatively) brief history of the concept of insight, beginning with work on creativity and problem solving in the early 1900's, then transitioning through the Gestalt approaches of the mid 1900's and through to the research currently being done by brain scan researchers around the world. I end the chapter by sharing my own working definition of insight and by introducing the three major types of insight that seem to exist "in the wild" (i.e., outside the lab).

The information in this chapter provides a baseline understanding of what insight actually *is*, both in terms of its biological mechanics – and in terms of its phenomenological experience. This understanding provides a solid foundation for the steps of the Impasse to Insight Method that I present in all of the following chapters, and I will refer back to key concepts from this chapter throughout the rest of the book.

What Research Tells Us About the Nature of Insight

Our understanding of the concept of insight actually begins with some of the earliest work on creativity and problem solving, as articulated by Graham Wallas in his 1926 classic, *The Art of Thought*[2]. Wallas suggested that when trying to solve a problem, human beings work their way through several predictable stages. His original book postulated five stages, though most researchers today focus on only four of those stages.

The first stage is preparation – and this is the stage where most of the (conscious) work is done. This is when you clarify what the actual problem is and work diligently to solve it, using processes like logic and reasoning. If you find the solution to the problem during this stage, the rest of the stages are unnecessary and never kick in.

If, however, the problem is poorly defined and/or all your hard work to find an answer doesn't lead you to solution (i.e., you reach an impasse), the second stage is incubation. This is a period where you don't consciously think about the problem at all. This period of *not* consciously working on a problem (which can last for minutes or days or months or years) plays a powerful role in your ability to solve problems that have initially brought you to impasse.

The third stage in Wallas' original model (and the stage often dropped by current researchers) is "intimation," which essentially represents the feeling that you're "getting close" to the solution. It's like the children's game of "Hot and Cold," where one person hides an object and then lets the seeker know they're getting closer to discovering the hidden object by saying, "Warmer...warmer..." as the seeker gets physically closer to where the object is hidden. This "getting closer" feeling is essentially absent from modern understandings of insight experiences, where the hallmark of a true insight experience is the distinctive feeling that the solution springs out of nowhere. Multiple studies[3] have, in fact, demonstrated that feeling like you're "getting close" to a solution is *not* a good predictor of whether you actually arrive at the correct solution to insight problems. In fact, the more strongly you have that feeling, the more likely you are to produce the *wrong* answer to an insight problem.*

The fourth of Wallas' original stages is "illumination," which is the moment when the answer to the problem or challenge suddenly pops into your head. This corresponds to the phenomenological experience of "Aha!" or "Eureka!"

---

* By contrast, that "getting closer" feeling is a good predictor of whether you will produce the correct answer when you solve *analytic* problems.

From Archimedes to the Anterior Cingulate Cortex

The final stage in Wallas' model is "verification," which is where you test this newly found solution to see if it does, in fact, solve your original problem. If it doesn't, you then go back to the first (preparation) or second (incubation) stages and begin another cycle through the stages (do not pass Go, do not collect $200).

Building on Wallas' early work on creativity and problem solving, the next major players in the insight space (and the first to coin and use the term "insight" as we think of it today) were the Gestalt psychologists of the early- and mid-20th Century. The defining feature of the Gestalt school of insight is its focus (dare I say, "obsession") with the concept of "restructuring the problem." Citing Karl Duncker's seminal work, *On Problem Solving*[4], Richard E. Mayer[5] summarizes the Gestalt position on insight by stating that, "[w]hat is really done in any solution of problems consists in formulating the problem more productively."

Even many of the researchers who are currently doing extremely complex and technical experiments on the neural indicators of insight using EEG and fMRI equipment continue to define insight in the Gestalt "problem restructuring" tradition. For example, the very first paragraph of a *PLOS ONE* research study from Simone Sandkühler and Joydeep Bhattacharya[6] defined insightful problem solving as having four key components: "(i) mental impasse; (ii) restructuring of the problem representation, which leads to (iii) a deeper understanding of the problem, and finally culminates in (iv) an 'Aha!' feeling of suddenness and obviousness of the solution."

Essentially, the core belief of researchers in the Gestalt tradition is that insight isn't the moment when you suddenly realize the *solution* to a problem – it's the moment when you suddenly realize that the way you had been thinking about the *problem* is all wrong. As soon as you realize what the problem actually is, the solution essentially becomes self-evident and all is right with the world once again. Even though it *feels* like what you're struggling with is the lack of solution to your problem, what you're *really* struggling with is the fact that you're not thinking about the problem in the right way, so you're doomed to be stuck at an impasse until you can fix your framing of the problem. Once you get that sorted out, the solution pretty much takes care of itself.

In the spirit of full disclosure, I have some problems with the Gestalt approach to defining insight. I think that it's absolutely true that sometimes the reason why we get stuck as we wrestle with a problem is because we're not thinking about the problem in the right way. We may have misinterpreted some of the information, or we may be unnecessarily restricting the options we think we can consider, or we just may not be seeing the situation very clearly. And in those cases, if we can suddenly realize that the problem we're working on isn't really the problem at all – it's this other thing over here to the side instead – then I do think that can lead to a solution and rapid resolution of the (real) problem.

However, I don't think this is the *only* way that insight works. It's certainly been my own experience (and the experience of many people I worked with as I wrote this book) that sometimes, the problem you think you're facing is, in fact, the actual problem. The issue isn't that I'm thinking about the problem incorrectly; the problem is that I am totally clueless as to what the solution to this problem is. Or I'm faced with a very difficult decision that I have to make, and I'm genuinely struggling to determine which of my options is best.

After several decades of dominance, the Gestalt approach began to be challenged by a quite different perspective on the nature of insight – which is the belief that there essentially is no such thing as insight at all. This school of thought has taken the position that there is "nothing new" or "nothing unique" about insight as compared to other forms of problem-solving. Mayer[7] refers to a series of studies by Robert Weisberg[8] in which he concluded that "there seems to be very little reason to believe that solutions to novel problems come about in flashes of insight" and that, instead, people merely "create solutions to new problems by starting with what they know and later modifying it to meet the specific problem at hand."

In this view of the world, "insight" as we think about it – a sudden awareness of a totally new idea, or totally new way of combining things, or totally new way of seeing the world – basically doesn't exist. There's nothing new under the sun – there's just taking what you already know from past experience and tweaking it as necessary to address whatever the current problem happens to be.

Personally, I simply cannot accept the position that there's "nothing new" or "nothing unique" about the process of – and experience of – insight. There's just too much evidence to support insight as a distinct mental process. And, equally important, the experience of insight simply *feels* too different and distinct from more routine or analytic problem solving not to be a separate and unique (though certainly related) phenomenon. The research doesn't support the "nothing new" theory – and neither does the phenomenological experience of insight. So, although I've included it here for completeness, it won't get any more attention.

The final group of insight researchers operating today isn't held together by a shared belief about the specific definition of insight at all – they're held together by their methods of studying insight, however they may individually define it. These are the brain researchers, and they're at the forefront of current academic work in this space.

What the Brain Tells Us About the Nature of Insight

Warning: Very cool (and mildly complex) technical concepts and language ahead.

Just like certain drugs have warning labels on them, I feel I should include a mild "heads-up" for this section, which focuses on insight research conducted primarily using a variety of sophisticated brain scanning technologies. Where appropriate, I've included some brief quotes from research studies that nicely summarize key findings – and there's no getting around the fact that some of the jargon used in these journal articles is pretty highfalutin'. In cases where the "official" explanation offered by the original study authors seems particularly dense, I've included my own "Translation to Regular English" to help make the concepts more accessible.

Generally speaking, the researchers working in the brain neuroimaging space believe that there *is* something truly unique about insight and that it is distinct from more general problem-solving techniques, particularly more structured analytic problem-solving approaches. A study by Subramaniam, Kounios, Parrish and Jung-Beeman[9] did a beautiful job of summarizing the differences between insight and analytic problem-solving: "A plethora of behavioral evidence details how these two solving processes differ. Analytic processing involves deliberate application of strategies and operations to gradually approach solution. Insight, which is considered a type of creative cognition, is the process through which people suddenly and unexpectedly achieve solution through processes that are not consciously reportable. Insight solutions tend to involve conceptual reorganization, often occurring after solvers overcome an impasse in their solving effort, and are suddenly able to recognize distant or atypical relations between problem elements that had previously eluded them."

There are several key things to notice in this distinction between analytic and insightful problem solving. The first is that they are separate and distinct approaches. This isn't to say that they can't inform each other or that you can't use a combination of the two – just that there *are* two approaches, and that they differ. The second thing to note is that whereas analytic problem solving is methodical and incremental (so, basically, as you work on the problem you get closer and closer to the solution in increments until finally you arrive there), insight solutions tend to feel as if they spring out of nowhere. You're working and working on a problem, not feeling as though you're getting any closer to a solution, when – BAM! – the solution pops into your head in an instant. Zero to sixty in no seconds flat.

One other very interesting thing to note in the Subramaniam et al.[10] article is that the thought processes that lead to insight are generally "not consciously reportable." Needless to say, this presents enormous problems for anyone trying to research and understand insight (yours truly included). If the person who's just had an insight can't actually tell you how they came to have the insight...well, let's just say that it makes the research process a whole lot more interesting. One of the things it leads to is researchers moving away from relying exclusively on what their *subjects* tell them – and more on what subjects' *brains* tell them.

Without question, the hottest research approaches in the insight space these days involve brain scan studies – generally some combination of electroencephalogram (EEG) and functional magnetic resonance imaging (fMRI). Both approaches involve recording changes in different regions of the brain as the subject participates in an experiment on insight-related decision making. The beauty of these studies is that although we as human beings may not be able to consciously identify and verbalize how our brains are solving insight problems, the EEG and fMRI machines allow us to essentially "cut out the middleman" (i.e., the subject him or herself) and "talk" directly to the brain and see what it can tell us about what's going on in our heads as we tackle these problems.

I should preface this discussion by noting a couple of things. First, there is not universal agreement among brain-scan researchers as to exactly which areas of the brain "light up" as people solve problems via insight. It's also worth noting that there are not just differences in brain region involvement during the actual solution-search process; studies have also demonstrated that the states our brains are in as we *prepare* to receive a challenge bias us either towards arriving at the solution via insight or via more analytic methods. So before we even have a specific problem in front of us, the state our brain is in has already started us down either an insight-friendly or an analytic-friendly path without us being aware of it.

Specifically, prior to the presentation of problems that end up being solved via insight, there tends to be "greater neural activity over the temporal lobes of both cerebral hemispheres (i.e., around the ears) and over the mid-frontal cortex,"[11] specifically the anterior cingulate cortex (ACC). Researchers postulate that the activation of the right and left temporal lobes "suggest priming of the brain areas that process lexical and semantic information"[12] (i.e., the parts of the brain that understand language and assign meaning to things, particularly words and symbols). Based on other neuroimaging studies that implicate the anterior cingulate cortex in various cognitive control processes, scientists hypothesize that "the anterior cingulate may be involved in the readiness to detect weakly activated, subconscious solutions and to switch attention to them when they are detected."[13] Essentially, this pattern of preparatory activation seems to prime our brains to test and make meaning of the words and symbols we're about to see – and to be on the lookout for non-obvious connections between things. Kounios and Beeman[14] suggest that this pattern represents essentially an inward directing of attention.

By contrast, the brain region that seems to define preparatory states that lead to *analytic* solutions appears to be the posterior (or visual) cortex.[15] The hypothesis here is that this activation reflects a greater "amount of visual information passed along to higher cortical areas." Kounios and Beeman[16] interpret this as an indication that participants are "directing attention outwardly – that is, to the monitor on which the next problem [is] about to be displayed."

Taken together, all this research suggests that the patterns of brain activation that characterize the pre-*analytic* preparatory phase are ones that focus on external stimuli ("the solution is *out there* somewhere"). By contrast, the patterns of brain activation that characterize the pre-*insight* preparatory phase are ones that focus on internal awareness ("the solution is *in here* somewhere").

Of course, there aren't just differences in the states that *precede* the act of solving a problem via insight versus via more analytic methods – there are differences in the brain activation patterns *during* the actual problem solving as well. An excellent (if incredibly dense) review of the past ten years of neuroimaging studies in the insight field conducted by a trio of Chinese researchers nicely summarizes current understanding of the key brain areas involved in insight, and they use the term "the insightful brain" to refer to the group of involved structures:

"This putative framework is not an independent structural entity, but it is a neural network that is constructed by the distributed brain regions and neural substances and the neural connections between the distributed brain regions. The insightful brain involves many distributed brain regions, including the lateral prefrontal cortex, cingulate cortex (primarily the ACC and PCC), hippocampus, superior temporal gyrus, fusiform gyrus, precuneus, cuneus, insula, cerebellum and some areas of the parietal cortex." [17]

Translation to Regular English:

There isn't one specific area of the brain that is responsible for the experience of insight; instead, insight seems to be the result of a lot of different parts of the brain working together in very precise and well-coordinated ways. Unlike something like fear, which can be pinpointed as originating in a very specific (and very ancient) part of the brain – the amygdala – insight, by contrast, involves a bunch of different areas of the brain, including many parts that are involved in sophisticated types of "higher thinking" or cognition. If you want to use a musical analogy, fear would be someone blasting a single musical note as loudly as possible on a trumpet – and insight would be an entire symphony orchestra playing Beethoven's "Ode to Joy."

Looking at the illustration below (Figure 1), you can see just how widespread the areas involved in insight actually are.

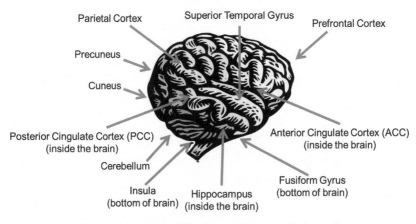

Figure 1: Areas of the brain that are believed to be involved in insight-driven problem solving.

Eve Grodnitzky

Shen et al.[18] go on to explain the hypothesized role that each of these brain areas plays in the insight process. I say "hypothesized" because although researchers understand to a degree what the main role of each of these brain areas is, its contribution to the insight process specifically is tentative at best at this point. Different researchers have different beliefs about what the phenomenon of insight actually is, and so brain region X, Y or Z lighting up might be interpreted by one researcher as meaning one thing – and by another researcher as meaning something else. Bearing that in mind, here is what Shen and colleagues have abstracted as the likely roles of the various brain regions:

"The lateral prefrontal cortex is responsible for the mental set shift in insight problem solving. The cingulate cortex is involved in cognitive conflicts between new and old ideas and progress monitoring, and the hippocampus, superior temporal gyrus and fusiform gyrus form an integrated functional network that specializes in the formation of novel and effective associations. The effective transformation of problem representation depends on a non-verbal visuospatial information-processing network that comprises the precuneus and cuneus and other regions that are distributed in the parietal-occipital junction. The insula reflects cognitive flexibility and the emotional experience that is associated with insight."[19]

Translation to Regular English:

The lateral prefrontal cortex is responsible for allowing us to switch between different problem-solving strategies and possible solutions as we search for the right answer. The cingulate cortex helps us figure out whether to hold on to old ideas or swap them out for new ones, and it gives us a sense of whether we're moving in the right direction or not. The hippocampus, superior temporal gyrus and fusiform gyrus work together to mix-and-match ideas from all over our brains in an attempt to find the combination of things that will trigger an insight. The precuneus, cuneus and various regions in the parietal-occipital junction are in charge of taking visual inputs (i.e., stuff we see) and translating that information into useful ways of thinking about (and possibly changing our framing of) the problem. The insula has two critical roles to play: (1) ensuring we remain open to other/better options as we try to solve the problem and (2) providing the emotional "Eureka!" or "Aha!" experience of surprise and/or joy we have at the moment of insight itself.

As if all this wasn't enough, there's also some evidence to suggest that there is a hemispheric component to insight, with more overall activation of the right hemisphere seen during insight solutions and more activation of the left hemisphere seen during analytic solutions. This is hypothesized to reflect the fact that the left hemisphere seems to be better at identifying strong and specific connections between things – and the right hemisphere is better at identifying weak and diffuse connections between things. Because insight tends to result from the identification of weak and/or non-obvious connections, the diffuse attention strategy favored by the right hemisphere may contribute to the solution of problems via insight.[20]

Last but not least, I would be remiss if I closed out this section on brain research without acknowledging that one of the challenges when attempting to study insight in the lab is the fact that there's not universal agreement as to what counts as an "insight problem" in the lab. As a result, there's rather wide variety in the challenges that subjects are asked to tackle when they're hooked up to EEG and fMRI machines. Not surprisingly, different problems and methodologies can lead to differences in which parts of the brain seem to be involved in problem preparation and solution. That said, there are two methodologies that are dominant in the academic world these days, largely dictated by geography/nationality (i.e., Chinese versus non-Chinese). I describe them here in some detail because references to them will appear in various studies throughout the book.

There's a considerable amount of research being done by Chinese researchers both inside and outside of China these days, and these researchers generally tend to prefer the "Chinese logograph" version of insight problems. Among non-Chinese researchers, the dominant approach is to use "remote associates test" (aka "RAT") problems. Or, if you prefer the non-vermin nomenclature, "compound remote associates" (CRA) problems. The Chinese approach is more complicated to explain (at least to non-native Chinese speakers), so I'll start with that one.

For a detailed explanation of how Chinese logographs are used in laboratory settings, check out the *ScienceDirect* article "Neural correlates of the 'Aha' experiences: Evidence from an fMRI study of insight problem solving" by Jiang Qiu et al.,[21] available on the www.sciencedirect.com website. I'm grossly oversimplifying how it works, but essentially subjects are presented with a riddle (in Chinese) whose answer is a single Chinese character. To begin, subjects are given a sample riddle – and the answer to that riddle so they see how it works. Then they're given the actual experimental riddle and asked to come up with the answer to that one on their own.

In the literature, the most often-cited practice riddle translates roughly as "having a mouth but being unable to speak" – the answer to which is the Chinese character meaning "mute." With Chinese logographs, the idea is that the solution is generally a clever combination of elements found within the riddle itself; basically, if you break apart the characters in the riddle, you can combine a couple of them to come up with the solution. The solution is hidden somewhere within the original riddle, and the challenge is to find it.

Once subjects have been given the practice riddle and the answer (so they get the hang of it), they're then given the actual "test" or "target" riddle – and asked to figure out the solution to that one on their own. An often-cited target riddle roughly translates as "having eyes but being unable to see." The solution to that riddle would be the Chinese character for "blind," which again is essentially hidden or embedded in characters that make up the riddle itself (I'm assuming that this is a lot more difficult in Chinese than it appears to be in the English translation).

The approach to finding the solution can be analytic-based (i.e., running through a bunch of different options in your head and ruling things out as you go) or insight-based (i.e., the solution just suddenly pops into your head). As soon as subjects solve each of the problems, they're immediately asked to indicate whether they arrived at each solution via insight or not. Researchers can then go back and look at the differences in brain scans that were recorded for insight solutions and non-insight solutions, with the goal being to see which parts of the brain fire (or stop firing) when people arrive at the solution via insight.

The other dominant methodology these days – used by pretty much everyone except researchers working with native Chinese speakers – is the "compound remote associates" (CRA) approach (aka the "RAT" or "remote associates test"). The CRA approach flashes a set of three words on a computer screen (e.g., crab, pine, sauce) and asks participants to come up with a single word that could be combined with each of the three target words to form a viable compound word or familiar two-word phrase. In the current example, the correct answer would be "apple" because you can combine it with the three original words to make "crabapple," "pineapple" and "applesauce."[22] Just like the Chinese logogriph riddles, CRA problems can be solved either through insight or through more analytic processes, and after giving the answer to each challenge, subjects are asked to indicate if they came up with the answer to that specific challenge via insight or not. Once again, researchers can then look at the brain scans corresponding to each individual challenge and determine which parts of the brain were firing (or not firing) during insight trials and during non-insight trials.

As mentioned earlier in this section, although there is still debate as to exactly which parts of the brain fire (or stop firing) both before and during insight problem solving, the vast majority of brain researchers do at least agree on one thing – and that is the fact that something very different happens when we solve problems via insight...and that something begins before we're even confronted with the problem itself.

Eve Grodnitzky

Nature Loves Variety – and So Does Insight

As we have seen, researchers in the insight space often have quite different criteria for what counts as "insight" (everything from the Gestalt obsession with "restructuring the problem" to folks who consider it "just an extension of general problem-solving skills"). Nevertheless, each school of thought does come up with a fairly narrow definition of insight in the end. So in every approach, insight tends to be this one tiny, very specific thing. Granted, some of this is a function of academic writing, which tends by its nature to be…let's call it…"detail-oriented." Whatever the reason, insight is most often defined in a way that makes it sound like an incredibly exclusive club that's virtually impossible to get into.

Personally, I find the country club approach far too restrictive – and not a good match to the variety of ways that we actually experience insight in our personal and professional lives. I think of insight more like color – where there is the prototypical "green" that we all probably think of when asked to imagine that color, but where there are lots of other variations on that color that also count as "green." So if I open one of those magical boxes of Crayola® crayons (the deluxe 64-count box with the sharpener in the back), I might pick the crayon labeled plain old "Green" if asked to identify the "most typical green" in the box. But I would also identify as green the crayons labeled "Asparagus" and "Forest Green" and "Sea Green" and "Olive Green" and "Granny Smith Apple" – and probably even "Yellow Green."

Just like green has many different shades, so does insight – and all of those shades can provide us with the profound mind shifts that change how we work and live. At the highest level, I think there are three categories of insight that seem to make the most sense. Returning to the color analogy, we've got the greenish greens, the bluish greens and the yellowish greens. They're all green – just different variations on the theme.

Bearing all of this in mind – and recognizing that all the laboratory-based studies of insight have only just begun to chip away at the very outer edges of our understanding of the phenomenon – I feel at liberty to put forward my own definition of insight, which is the one that I'll use throughout this book. My strategy is to take a rather more inclusive approach to insight than is generally taken in academic circles. My reason for this is that the myriad ways we actually experience insight *in real life* seem to be far more rich and diverse than the rather sterile experiences that tend to occur in the lab.

I think of it this way. I'm sure that you can create a synthetic rose smell in the lab whose chemical signature is exactly the same as a real rose – but it won't smell the same. Maybe it should – but it doesn't. It's precisely the same thing with insight. The fact of the matter is that insight as it occurs in real life bears an imperfect resemblance to what's considered insight in the lab, and it's insight in real life – in all its complexities and nuances and power – that I'm interested in. This book is about insight "in the wild" – and, as such, I've taken a broad perspective on what it includes.

Personally, I think of insight as: *the often sudden realization of a new truth or solution that is so obviously correct that there cannot be any question as to its veracity – and that is typically accompanied by a powerful emotional charge.* I didn't understand X…but now I suddenly do. I was unable to make this difficult decision…but now I see the right choice. I used to believe this thing was true…but now I believe something totally different. All of these are examples of the fundamental mind shifts that characterize insight. Looking across all the different types of insights that occur "in the wild" (i.e., in real life, outside the lab), three meta-categories emerge: (1) The Eureka Moment, (2) The Moment of Reckoning and (3) The Tectonic Shift, each of which I describe in more detail below.

The Eureka Moment

The "greenish greens" of insight are those experiences that we recognize as "Eureka Moments" or "Aha Moments" or "Light Bulb Moments." We're struggling to understand something that we simply can't get our minds around – or struggling to find a solution to a problem that seems to have none. We've worked the issue until we fear our brains are going to explode – but to no avail. We've reached an impasse. We're stuck.

And then suddenly – seemingly out of nowhere – the understanding or solution appears in our minds, often in surprisingly complete form. We go from being utterly clueless to having near-total clarity about the entire situation. There is a sense of rightness and certainty about the understanding or solution. The impasse has vaporized and we're unstuck. There's often a sense of "Oh, this is so obvious! How could I not have seen it before??" There's also usually a very specific physiological reaction – almost a physical jolt combined with a sense of excitement or awe ("OMG!" or "Whoa…").

The Moment of Reckoning

When we think of the "greenish green" of the Eureka Moment, we tend to think about situations where we start out as utterly clueless – and have either an infinite variety of options to choose from, or none at all. The "bluish greens" of insight – what I call "Moments of Reckoning" – are a sister phenomenon to the greenish green Eureka Moment. In a Moment of Reckoning, you're faced with the choice between a limited number of usually quite well-defined options – and you're absolutely stumped as to which choice is the optimal one. Whereas the time leading up to a Eureka Moment can make you feel inept as you struggle to come up with any solution or understanding, wrestling with a Moment of Reckoning can be far more tortuous as you try to figure out the mental regression equation that will maximize the upside and minimize the downside of the two or three (or more) seemingly viable options you're considering.

Moments of Reckoning often remind me of the old game show "Let's Make a Deal," where one of the games required the contestant to choose whether s/he wanted what was behind either Door #1 or Door #2 or Door #3. Behind one of those doors there was a fabulous prize – and behind the other two doors, there were sad, pathetic little prizes. Your job as a contestant was to figure out which door to pick so that you got the awesome prize rather than one of the crummy ones. The "Moment of Reckoning" insight experience is much the same. You're standing there looking at a bunch of seemingly identical closed doors, trying your best to figure out which one to pick – and feeling like you don't have enough information to make a good choice. So you often get stuck in an endless loop of mentally debating each of your options and end up paralyzed, unable to make any choice at all, for fear that it will be the wrong one. Generally speaking, when insight into the best choice does finally appear, the primary feelings will be relief and resolution ("Thank heaven all that dithering is over – now let's get on with it!"). It's as if the pressure of a huge amount of water has built up behind a dam – and suddenly the dam gives way. The tension is released and all the built-up energy surges forward.

The Tectonic Shift

The yellowish green of insight is a phenomenon that I think of as the "Tectonic Shift" – and it's a different kind of animal from the first two types. For starters, its influence is often much broader. Whereas Eureka Moments and Moments of Reckoning generally focus on insights into very specific challenges, Tectonic Shifts often operate at a more global level, altering how we see the world much more broadly. They're also the only one of the insight types that can appear spontaneously (often in response to the most unexpected of stimuli), rather than being a deliberate response to a specific challenge or problem (though you can certainly put them to use against a specific challenge or problem after the fact).

Again, while not discounting the fact that you certainly can make deliberate efforts to change your perspective on big issues, in my experience the most powerful Tectonic Shifts sneak up on you when you least expect it and when you're not aware that there's anything wrong with the way you currently see and experience the world. You're going through life as you always do, and then – BAM! – something happens to jolt you out of your comfortable little bubble and you suddenly see the world and/or yourself in an entirely new light. In this way, they're very much like the earthquake-related phenomenon that their name derives from, when two of the Earth's plates suddenly slip against each other and shake things up in (sometimes) alarming ways. For the most part, you never see them coming, but they can seriously rock your world.

Tectonic Shifts are also a bit different in their timing. They certainly can be sudden flashes of clarity that seem to come out of nowhere like Eureka Moments and Moments of Reckoning – but they can also come in gradual, incremental forms where they gain momentum over time before building to a crescendo. As a result, phenomenologically, they can feel either like a bolt of lightning out of the blue – or like the slow rise of dawn. Both result in illumination; it's just that the time scales are quite different. Much like the physics of plate tectonics, although the earthquake (or insight) feels sudden and relatively brief when it finally arrives, the pressure that had to build up for that shift to occur can take quite some time to accumulate.

One Final Thought

One other thing to note is that although I talk about the three types of insight as if they're distinct phenomena (mostly for the sake of clarity/ease), there are elements of overlap among them. Also bear in mind that an insight experience doesn't have to be limited to a single category, either. You can face a challenge, hit an impasse and then have a Eureka Moment that breaks you out of that impasse – and then that Eureka Moment, as you reflect on it over time, can lead to a Tectonic Shift. So although the three different types of insight do reflect useful ways to talk about the different variations of insight experiences, try not to interpret them so strictly that they become more limiting than they are helpful.

So What?

Why is it important to understand what insight is and how our understanding of it has evolved over time? There are a couple of reasons. The first is that there's considerable variation in how the term "insight" is used these days – to mean everything from "a good idea" to "an understanding" to "an epiphany." As I use the term in this book, insight is *the often sudden realization of a new truth or solution that is so obviously correct that there cannot be any question as to its veracity – and that is typically accompanied by a powerful emotional charge.* It is, in essence, the discovery of an unexpected and blinding truth that blows your mind. Insights have tremendous potential to be life's great game-changers because they not only reveal a new – and irrefutable – truth, but because they provide the emotional jolt that drives us to act upon this revelation.

It is also important to understand that insight is, in fact, a distinct phenomenon from such things as analytic problem-solving, creativity and innovation. Not only does the experience of insight feel different, brain scan research has repeatedly demonstrated that it *is* different – both in terms of the preparatory states that are conducive to insight and in terms of the brain's behavior during actual insight problem solving. Therefore, it is important to extend our understanding beyond what we already know about the mechanics of creativity, innovation and more generalized problem solving. Understanding how these phenomena work is not sufficient to understand how to facilitate and accelerate genuine insight generation in our personal and professional lives, though they are certainly good starting points.

The Impasse to Insight Method that I describe in the remainder of this book builds upon existing understandings of these related phenomena, plus the (somewhat more limited) current academic understanding of insight itself. Combined with a qualitative analysis of hundreds of real-life insight experiences, the approach provides a methodology that individuals, teams and organizations can use to both facilitate and accelerate insight generation.

CHAPTER 2

Mind the Gap:
Clearly Define the Problem Statement

My husband Gustavo and I are fortunate enough to live in the mountains outside of Denver, Colorado. When we were searching for what would become our home here, we spent nearly a year "boiling the ocean" in our search for just the right house. We'd had multiple conversations – with each other and with our real estate agent – about the specific list of criteria we were looking for (and exactly what we didn't want). And yet, after months and months of online searching, plus in-person visits to more than thirty houses that were carefully selected because they appeared to meet our criteria – we still hadn't found anything that was even remotely awesome enough for us to pick up and move halfway across the country.

There was the house that had a perfect floor plan – but an uninspiring setting. And the "cathedral house" with stained glass windows and a great yard for the dogs – but an astonishingly odd layout when visited in person. And the house that we placed an (accepted) offer on – that was snatched out from under us at the last minute by a weasel-like member of "The Mountain Mafia" real estate team that owns most of the market in these parts.

Finally, after walking through – and being disappointed by – yet another supposedly promising house nearly a year into the search process, we were beginning to despair that we'd ever find a house that would make us (and our dogs and cats) truly happy. That evening, Gustavo and I sat down and tried to do a bit of a root cause analysis on why none of the houses that supposedly met all our criteria were "The One." And what we realized was that if none of these "perfect match" houses felt right… then maybe we had our criteria wrong.

Immediately, we got to work on reviewing what really was (and wasn't) important to us, particularly in light of things we'd liked and disliked in all the previous houses we'd seen. As it turned out, some things were critically more important than we'd initially thought – and other things were significantly less so. For Gustavo, the one absolute non-negotiable was a view. And not just any view, but a view that said, "You are in Colorado, and there can be no mistaking it for anywhere else on earth." For me, my one non-negotiable was a yard that was fetch-friendly for the dogs. Anything that was too small or too steep for an afternoon of enthusiastic doggie games was a no-go. Because, as experience has taught me, "a tired dog is a good dog."

With our revised criteria in mind, we began a new search – and, lo and behold, we almost immediately found a house that was even more perfect for us (and the dogs and cats!) than we could have dreamed of. I'm sitting in my office in that house as I type this sentence, looking out at the pine trees rustling in the wind as a thunderstorm rolls down the valley and tints the dark grey clouds with hints of pink. It's a situation and a view made possible only by the fact that we realized that our criteria for success – our problem statement, to use root cause analysis terminology – needed an overhaul. Once we got that right, everything else clicked into place like the pieces of a puzzle.

For the record, we still think The Mountain Mafia guy is a weasel, but we're grateful that his devious little manoeuver kept us out of the house we thought we wanted – and kept us looking for the house that really was "The One."

Mind the Gap

In a Nutshell

In the Impasse to Insight Method that I describe in this book, the first step towards facilitating and accelerating the insight-generation process is crafting a well-defined problem statement. Before I can come up with a brilliant solution, I need to have crystal clarity about what the actual problem is. To quote one of the masters of innovation and insight, Albert Einstein: "The mere formulation of a problem is far more often essential than its solution".[1] I'm not sure I would go quite so far as to suggest that a well-formed problem statement is *more* important than the actual solution to that problem – but it's close. We'll call it a tie.

In this chapter, I begin by making the case for a well-crafted problem statement and then go on to discuss two different approaches to crafting a problem statement: (1) the problem-focused variety and (2) the end-state focused variety. Both approaches are equally valid, and which approach you choose for any particular challenge will depend on whether it's easier to articulate (1) what's currently wrong or (2) what the ideal future state is.

I end the chapter by discussing the importance (and, perhaps, the inevitability) of reframing your problem statement as you progress through the steps of the Impasse to Insight Method and begin to gain a better understanding of the problem and its possible solution(s). As explained in Chapter 1, although Gestalt psychologists consider problem reframing to actually *be* insight itself, my perspective (and the perspective of all non-Gestalt researchers) is that problem reframing is *part of the process* that gets you to insight, but it alone is not insight.

The Importance of Starting With a Solid Problem Statement

The first – and, in some ways, most important – step in the insight-generation process is "defining the problem statement." What this means is that before you can even begin to think about the moment of insight itself, you have to make sure you've got crystal clarity around what – exactly – you want to have an insight about. It sounds simple in theory, yet it can be quite challenging in practice. You have to boil it down to the essence of the *problem* – and weed out anything that is instead a possible *cause* or a possible *solution*. For example, this is *not* a good problem statement: "I need to fire Joe because his bad attitude is making everyone else on Team X miserable and destroying the group's quarterly results." In that single sentence you've got a mishmash of problems (bad quarterly results), causes (Joe's bad attitude and Team X's misery) and solutions (I need to fire Joe). A problem statement must focus *only* on the actual problem at hand, so you have to weed out everything else in order to have a strong jumping-off point for the insight-generation process.

Bearing that in mind, this would be a far better version of this particular problem statement: "Team X is consistently missing their quarterly performance targets." You'll notice that this second version of the statement eliminates all the assumptions, possible causes and possible solutions that clouded the original version of the statement. Now that it is a nice, clear articulation of the problem, it can serve as a good foundation for the insight-generation process.

Types of Problem Statements

Just like there are several types (or "shades," if we want to go back to our color analogy) of insight, there are also a couple of types of possible problem statements that we can utilize in the insight-generation process: (a) the problem-focused variety and (b) the end-state-focused variety. The problem-focused variety is the more traditional version of a problem statement. The goal of this type of problem statement is to articulate as clearly and succinctly as possible *what is currently wrong*. Examples of a problem-focused statement might be: "Our stock price is in the toilet" or "My cholesterol is dangerously high" or "We can't retain our high-performing employees" or "My dog pees on the carpet if I leave her alone for more than an hour." Each of these problem statements frames the issue at hand in terms of what currently sucks.

By contrast, the end-state-focused version of a problem statement focuses not on what's currently wrong – but on what the *desired future state is*. Examples of an end-state-focused problem statement might be: "We need to double our revenues in the next five years" or "I want to fit into my favorite jeans again" or "We need a slate of ready-now successors for the entire C-suite by the end of the year" or "I want to be able to bench press 300 pounds." Note that although each statement sort of implies a current (undesirable) state, the focus is instead on the happy place that we're ultimately trying to get to, rather than the suboptimal place we are now.

Really, it's two sides of the same coin, as each type of problem statement either directly or indirectly addresses both current and future state. It's just that sometimes it's easier to figure out "what currently sucks" (problem-focused variety) and sometimes it's easier to figure out "what would be awesome in the future" (end-state-focused variety). Either approach works, so you just need to pick the one that you can articulate most clearly.

The Benefits of Pressure-Testing (and Possibly Reframing) Your Problem Statement

There are a couple of things to keep in mind here. The first is that if you're genuinely looking to apply the Impasse to Insight Method to solve a problem or make a decision or bring about a broad tectonic shift, then (ideally) you should not progress to the next step in the Method until you have totally nailed the problem statement. There's no sense going to all the effort to have a major breakthrough if it's not going to address the problem that you're truly trying to solve. You can certainly keep reading this book so that you have a sense of the complete process – just bear in mind that when it comes to application, you'll want to fully articulate your problem statement before moving on to any of the subsequent steps.

The other thing to bear in mind is that it is most definitely possible that your problem statement will evolve as you progress through the steps of the Impasse to Insight Method. As you start to make new connections between things and think about the issues and possibilities differently, it's not uncommon to find yourself needing to reframe the problem a bit.

Something along the lines of "Gosh, I thought the problem was X...but now I recognize that the real problem is Y!"

In fact, as discussed in the previous chapter, Gestalt psychologists (who have heavily influenced research in the insight space) believe that "reframing the problem" actually *is* insight. They suggest that the "Eureka!" experience isn't the moment when you discover a previously hidden solution to your problem – it's the moment when you reframe your problem in a new way that also implies its solution.

In their 2008 article on the cognitive abilities involved in insight problem solving, DeYoung, Flanders and Peterson gave this notion of redefining the problem statement an interesting twist.[2] They wrote that problems in general can be divided into two broad classes: well-defined problems and poorly-defined problems. In a well-defined problem, it's clear what the current state is, what the desired end state is and what the rules of engagement are for getting from the current state to the end state. As a result, one should be able to make steady ("if not certain") progress towards that goal. If progress – or ultimate success – isn't achieved, then it's likely due to a lack of relevant skill, effort or information on the part of the problem solver, and not a fault of the problem statement itself.

As DeYoung and his colleagues point out, this is all very well and good in the lab and in the classroom, where most problems used for testing are well-defined.[3] Alas, in real life, problems are usually poorly defined, which is another kettle of fish entirely.

In poorly defined problems, not only is there uncertainty about whether you'll be able to achieve the goal – there are often questions about what the actual goal is, what the current state is and what's possible in terms of the methods one can employ to get from the current state to the end state. When there's this much uncertainty, the most productive first step you can take in your attempts to solve the problem is to try to turn the poorly defined problem into a well-defined problem.[4] As such, the Gestalt concept of "reframing the problem" likely plays a critical role; the clearer your understanding of all the elements of the problem, the more successful your problem-solving efforts are likely to be.

Mind the Gap

Whether or not you embrace the Gestalt definition of insight (full disclosure: I think that it's just one of the ways insight works in the real world), the first step in your insight-generation efforts should always be crafting a concise problem statement that accurately reflects the true problem at hand. Bear in mind that if the challenge all along (unbeknownst to you, of course) has been that you've been thinking about the problem in a sub-optimal way, once you get a better formulation of the problem, the solution may be obvious to you. If that's the case, then congratulations, you don't need to go through most of the rest of the steps in the insight-generation process and can skip directly to implementation of your insight (Chapter 8).

Sadly, it's usually not that easy. More often than not, you'll find that although you can significantly improve upon your original formulation of the problem (and you should!), reframing the problem statement generally doesn't magically and immediately present you with a solution. As a result, once you've got your revised problem statement, the next thing you'll need to do to accelerate and facilitate the insight-generation process is identify and remove any blockers to your insight-generation success, which is the focus of the next chapter.

So What?

Just like a journey of a thousand miles begins with a single step, so does the process of insight generation. What's critically important to realize, however, is that if your first step is in the wrong direction, your journey is going to end up being a lot longer than a thousand miles. A well-defined problem statement sets the direction for your insight-generation journey and ensures that you begin pointed in the correct direction. For the Impasse to Insight Method to work efficiently, it is critically important that you start with a well-defined problem statement that specifies exactly what you're looking to have an insight about. You can approach problem statement creation from one of two directions ("what currently sucks" or "what the ideal future state would be"), but either way, you need to begin the insight-generation process with crystal clarity about exactly what sort of insight you're looking for.

Bear in mind that as you progress through the stages of the Impasse to Insight Method, your problem statement will likely evolve in response to additional things you learn along the way. The more you can refine your problem statement, the better – and, sometimes, those revisions themselves will be the catalyst for the insight they're designed to help you find.

CHAPTER 3

The Best Defense Is a Good Offense:
Proactively Identify and Remove Blockers to Insight

For the first time in all my years of teaching, it was starting to look like I was going to have to break up an actual fist fight in one of my sessions.

I was doing some in-house leadership development work with a major technology firm, and we had gotten to the point in the sessions where groups of executives were tasked with developing a solution to a very challenging new business development scenario. Their specific job in this part of the exercise was to figure out how to staff new stores devoted to a revolutionary new product line. Most of the teams were plugging away at fairly standard approaches to the problem – and getting along quite nicely with each other within their teams. One team, however, was virtually at each other's throats – a team that I would later affectionately refer to as "Team Phoenix."

The folks on this team couldn't agree on an approach (or anything else) and were all talking at and over each other, vying for control. As I visited their table yet again to see how things were going, one woman turned to me and said in an extremely exasperated voice, "I don't see the point in even creating these stores in the first place, let alone staffing them – it doesn't make any business sense." I replied, "Well, if this were a real situation in your business rather than a development exercise, what would you do?" She paused for a second and said, "Well, if the decision had already been made, I'd probably just do my best to execute on it – but if the decision *hadn't* been made yet, I'd make the case for doing something entirely different." I paused, smiled in a conspiratorial way, and quietly said to her and the rest of the team, "Go with that."

Instantly, the entire dynamic and energy of the team changed. Their eyes blazed to life and you could see them leaping out of their seats, heads together as they bent over the table, working collaboratively on their radical solution to the problem. There hadn't ever been anything in the instructions that specifically prohibited them from challenging the original strategic decision to open the new stores – but their assumption of this (non-existent) constraint had massively limited the options available to them. As soon as this imaginary constraint was eliminated, they sprang into action and – like a phoenix rising from the ashes – devised the most innovative (and dare I say most insightful) solution of any group I've ever worked with before or since.

In a Nutshell

This chapter and the following chapter are, in many ways, two sides of the same coin. Both are designed to set the stage for the success of your insight-generation efforts using the Impasse to Insight Method – it's just that this chapter focuses on *removing* stuff that hinders your efforts and the next chapter focuses on *adding* stuff that helps your efforts. Both are essential to setting yourself up for success in the subsequent steps.

Personally, I think it makes more sense to talk about wiping the slate clean of unhelpful stuff before turning your attention to adding things in, so this chapter focuses on how you identify and remove the things (and people) that could potentially block your insight-generation efforts. These blockers tend to fall into five categories, organized from the most internal of the challenges to the most external of the challenges. They are: (1) fixed mindsets, (2) functional fixedness, (3) unhelpful emotional states, (4) extraneous information, and (5) environmental blockers.

The Best Defense Is a Good Offense

The bad news is that the source of most of these problems is…you. As is so often the case in life, when it comes to insight generation, we are (unintentionally) our own worst enemies. The good news is that when you're the source of the problem, it's generally within your power to fix the problem.

As with most challenges, it's useful to begin by tackling some of the biggest, broadest problems you're likely to face, which in this case are the implications of a "fixed mindset."

Fixed Mindsets (Yours or Other People's)

Carol Dweck is a psychologist at Stanford University whose most well-known work[1] discusses the idea of "fixed mindsets" and "growth mindsets."* Every single one of us – adults and children alike – have a tendency towards one or the other of these mindsets. There are lots of reasons why we might develop one tendency versus the other that aren't specifically relevant here, but at any given point in our lives, we each have a tendency to be either more "fixed mindset" or "growth mindset" types (though – with effort – we can change which type we are).

In a nutshell, people with fixed mindsets believe that skills and abilities are essentially inherent – and, therefore, not really subject to change for better or worse. You are what you are, and there you have it. By contrast, people with growth mindsets believe that the skills and abilities you're born with (or that you have now) are just a starting point and are highly subject to change as a result of effort and learning. What's most relevant in the context of insight generation is the difference between what each mindset considers its top priority, which derives from the aforementioned fundamental beliefs.

The overriding priority for people with a fixed mindset is to "look smart at all costs." Fixed mindset folks also have a tendency to avoid challenges, give up easily, distain effort, fear feedback and resent the success of others.

---

* Dweck's book, *Mindset: The New Psychology of Success*, will rock your world, and I highly recommend you check it out.

People with fixed mindsets also tend to be quite judgmental – both of themselves and others. None of these tendencies are terribly helpful or adaptive in life, but it's really the issue of needing to "look smart at all costs" that causes the biggest problems for the insight-generation process. If this is your #1 priority, then experimentation, trial-and-error attempts, openness to other alternatives (the list goes on and on) simply are not an option. If you can't immediately come up with a brilliant solution to a challenge, you're likely to: (a) just go with whatever comes to mind ("Even a bad solution is better than admitting that I have no solution"); or (b) dismiss the suggestions of others ("If someone else has a better idea, it means I'm stupid and a failure"); or (c) give up entirely ("This is a dumb question and I'm not even going to bother with it").

One of the critical skillsets for success in the insight-generation process is the ability to hang out in a state of ambiguity for extended periods of time. You have to be OK with not knowing the right answer immediately, and you need to recognize that parts of the process will make you feel like you're stumbling around in the dark, desperately groping for a light switch. You also have to set aside the need to be right – and the even stronger fear of being wrong. These sorts of experiences make fixed mindset folks want to run screaming from the room – and I should know, as when I first read Dweck's book I realized (with genuine horror) that I fit the fixed mindset profile a lot better than the growth mindset profile. But, as they say, the first step is admitting you have a problem, and I've been clawing my way towards a growth mindset ever since.

Now contrast all of this with the growth mindset. The overriding priority for these folks is the "deep desire to learn." Beyond this, people with growth mindsets also tend to love challenges, persist in the face of setbacks, embrace effort, welcome feedback, and be inspired by the success of others. They're also relatively accepting of themselves and others (as opposed to judgmental). As a result, they're more than happy to engage in extensive experimentation and to consider alternatives other than their own. When they're working on an insight-generation challenge and they don't immediately have a brilliant solution, they don't get discouraged, settle for suboptimal solutions or resist the cool ideas of others. They recognize that insight generation is a process, and they're willing to feel kind of clueless for a while as they work through the steps that will lead to success. They're not so fixated on getting to the solution as quickly as possible that they can't enjoy (and fully capitalize on) the discovery process itself.

Recognizing that these two very different mindsets exist, your own first step in removing blockers to insight generation is to take a good, hard look at which mindset profile most closely matches your own. And you need to be honest, even if you don't like the answer (believe me, I feel your pain). And it's not just your own mindset that you have to be concerned with – it's the mindset of anyone else who's participating in the insight-generation process with you. If they bring fixed mindset baggage with them (look smart at all costs; avoid challenges; give up easily; distain effort; fear feedback; and resent the success of others) then you've got to drag that stuff out into the light and defuse it as much as possible. Even if you can't eliminate the issues entirely, you can at least make everyone aware of these maladaptive tendencies and try to nip them in the bud each time they rear their ugly little heads.

Functional Fixedness (and Other Unnecessary Constraints)

The second of the many ways that our own internal issues can impede our insight-generation efforts relates to the concept of functional fixedness and other limitations we put on ourselves and our options. Usually without even realizing it, we put more constraints on strategies and possible solutions than a situation itself truly requires. It's part of the mind's (well-intentioned, if not always terribly helpful) attempts to streamline the decision-making process.

A great example of this tendency in action is the classic "candle and tacks" insight problem first used by Adamson.[2] In "Condition A" of this experiment, a subject is brought into a room and placed in front of a table that's nestled up against a wooden or cork wall. On that table are a box of tacks, a candle, and a book of matches (Figure 1).

*Figure 1: Condition A with tacks **inside** the box.*

The subject is told that his or her job is to attach the candle to the wall above the table in such a way that, once the wick is lighted, the wax won't drip on the table. People fruitlessly try to solve this challenge in all sorts of ways, usually with no success whatsoever.

In "Condition B" of this experiment, subjects are given the exact same task, but with one small change. For these folks, the tacks aren't actually *in* the box, they're scattered on the table right next to the box (Figure 2).

*Figure 2: Condition B with tacks **outside** the box.*

The Best Defense Is a Good Offense

For most of these subjects, it takes relatively little time for them to realize that they can use the tacks to attach the box to the wall and then place the candle inside the box, thereby preventing the wax from dripping on the table (Figure 3).

Figure 3: Solution to the candle-and-tacks problem.

What this experiment demonstrates is the extent to which we can – inadvertently and without even knowing it – place constraints on our solution efforts. For the tacks-in-the-box people, they viewed the box only as a container for the tacks – and generally it didn't even occur to them that the box itself could be a player in the solution. Even if it did occur to them, they assumed (incorrectly) that the box wasn't fair game, even though there was nothing in the instructions that prevented them from using it. The instructions said that they could use "anything on the table" – and the box was "on the table" just like the tacks, candle and matches were.

The technical term for the challenges faced by the tacks-in-the-box subjects is *functional fixedness*[3] – and it means that we get so fixated (i.e., stuck) on the most obvious use for an object that we simply can't see other possibilities. Our (unintentional) obsession with seeing an object in one way blinds us to all other possibilities. This is a particular challenge when we're trying to solve a difficult problem, since if we're striving for insight, it probably means that the top one (or two or three) most obvious possible solutions aren't the right ones; if they were, we would have solved the problem immediately and been done with it. Although the term functional fixedness was originally designed to apply only to getting stuck on the dominant use (or "function") of a physical object, I tend to think of it more holistically as the problem that occurs whenever we get stuck thinking about *anything* in only one way (usually the most obvious or familiar or dominant way), whether it's a physical object, an idea, an emotion or anything else.

Functional fixedness is one of the key contributors to a state of impasse (i.e., not being able to progress any further) in the insight-generation process. Although we can certainly reach impasse simply because we've tried and exhausted all of the ideas that we're able to generate, more often than not, a big contributor to our state of impasse is functional fixedness. Even though we may not realize it, our brains have gotten stuck on one line of questioning or one avenue of solution search or one way of interpreting the problem and its constraints. As a result, we're stuck in an infinite "do loop," meaning that we're doing and thinking the same things over and over again rather than rejecting these unsuccessful approaches and searching out entirely new options. In these circumstances, it's hard not to reference a quote often attributed to Albert Einstein: "Insanity is doing the same thing over and over again...and expecting different results."

Also bear in mind that we can get stuck not only on a single (often erroneous) solution for the problem – but on a single (often erroneous) interpretation of the problem and its constraints as well. If you think back to the Team Phoenix example from the beginning of this chapter, you can see a clear example of how an overly narrow interpretation of the problem initially led them to a totally unsatisfying set of solution options. It was only when they realized that they'd inadvertently added in unnecessary limitations that they were able to break out of their narrow interpretation of the problem and, in turn, consider a whole bunch of different (and much cooler) solutions.

The Best Defense Is a Good Offense

What the concept of functional fixedness reminds us of is the extent to which we have to be vigilant against the encroachment of superfluous constraints on either our framing of the problem or the solutions we're willing and able to consider. Are we restricting ourselves unnecessarily? Do we have more latitude than we think we do? Are there options we've ruled out that we shouldn't have? Which of our assumptions warrant further pressure-testing? We must constantly be asking ourselves these questions both as we begin the insight-generation process and as we continue through it. Unwarranted constraints are very sneaky, and so we have to purposefully address these questions and make sure that they haven't managed to creep in through the back door when we weren't looking. There's a saying that "everything not specifically prohibited is allowed" – and I think this is a great mantra to keep in mind when trying to combat unnecessary constraints in the insight-generation process. Unless you have irrefutable evidence that something is not possible or viable – you should assume that it is.

Counterproductive Emotions

Whereas the challenges of a fixed mindset and functional fixedness are both internal and largely constant threats to our insight-generation efforts, the third of the possible obstacles is more fluid. It's still an internal challenge – but it's more mercurial, coming and going in response to innumerable factors, including the very nature of the problem we're trying to solve.

Sometimes, we're our own worst enemies when it comes to the insight-generation process. Any emotional baggage we're carrying around – whether it's about elements of the problem at hand, possible decisions or solutions implied by that problem, or just generalized stuff – can significantly interfere with our efforts. Although there are almost innumerable ways to get ourselves in trouble here, I consider "The Four Horsemen of the Emotional Apocalypse" to be fear, denial, guilt and anxiety. As you begin to work through the insight-generation process, you need to do an honest assessment of the extent to which these emotions are influencing your decisions and behaviors – and do everything in your power to limit the influence of the Four Horsemen.

Fear (noun): a distressing emotion aroused by impending danger, evil, pain, etc., whether the threat is real or imagined[4]

Denial (noun): a defense mechanism characterized by refusal to acknowledge painful realities, thoughts or feelings[5]

Guilt (noun): remorse or self-reproach caused by feeling that one is responsible for a wrong or offense[6]

Anxiety (noun): a state of uneasiness or tension caused by apprehension of possible future misfortune, danger, etc.; worry[7]

A special note on anxiety here. Of the Four Horsemen, anxiety is the one that has been most frequently studied in the insight literature, probably in part because science has a number of well-validated measures of anxiety, so we feel we can measure it effectively and reliably in the lab. But first, a couple of words about the related concept of "arousal" (in the totally G-rated sense, for the record), so that there's no confusion about the differential impacts of "arousal" versus "anxiety" when it comes to performance.

What we know from general studies of performance is that there's what's called an "inverted U-shaped" relationship between "arousal" and performance on most tasks (aka the Yerkes-Dodson Law). "Arousal" is essentially a measure of how fired up you feel, independent of whether it's a positive emotion (e.g., joy) or a negative emotion (e.g., fear) that's firing you up. A low arousal state would be when you're completely relaxed and at rest; a high arousal state would be when your body is essentially on "high alert" (which could be as a result of feeling extreme joy or intense fear or white-hot anger or any other number of intense emotions). Generally speaking, we perform best when we're in the "moderate arousal" zone – and worst when we're either at very low or very high levels of arousal (Figure 4).

The Best Defense Is a Good Offense

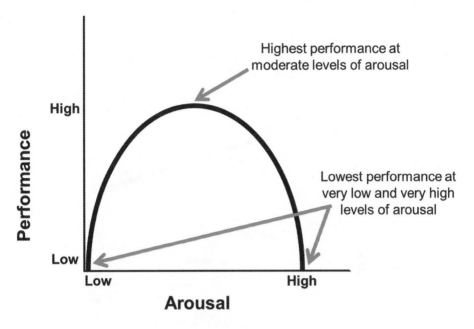

Figure 4: The Yerkes-Dodson Law: Moderate arousal often leads to better performance than low or high arousal.

However, when it comes to *anxiety*, the impact on performance is more complicated – especially when we look at performance specifically on insight problems. Anxiety has a clearly negative – and largely linear – effect on insight problem solving. In a nutshell, the more anxious you are, the less likely you are to be able to solve a problem via insight. A study by Subramaniam et al.[8] found that subjects who scored highest on various measures of anxiety consistently solved fewer CRA (compound remote associates) problems using insight than did subjects who scored the lowest on the anxiety measures. Interestingly, the high-anxiety folks made up (most of) the difference in *overall* problem-solving rates by instead employing more analytic strategies to solve the problems, but the reduction in their ability to solve problems via insight was dramatic (Figure 5).

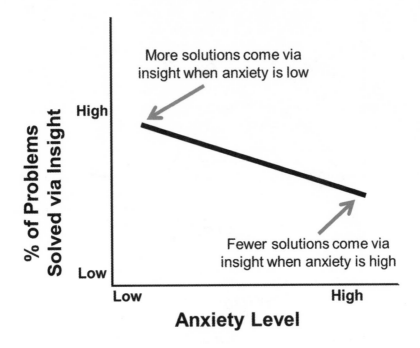

Figure 5: Lower anxiety levels lead to proportionally more solutions via insight.

Bearing these results (and others like them) in mind, if you're looking to solve a problem via insight, you'll want to be particularly aware of your levels of anxiety (both in general and with respect to the particular challenge you're facing) and take the necessary steps to manage that anxiety down as much as possible.

Anxiety and the other three Horsemen (fear, denial and guilt) can disrupt all stages of the insight-generation process, but you'll want to be particularly careful about how they interact with possible decisions or solutions – so, essentially, the outcomes of the insight-generation process. If you're anxious about what the results of your insight efforts might be, you're unlikely to get the real breakthrough you're looking for. If you feel guilty about what your moment of insight suggests, you're unlikely to realize its full power in execution.

The Best Defense Is a Good Offense

It's okay if you're concerned about the problem you're facing – in fact, you can put that energy to use as a motivator to drive you through the insight-generation process (and remember the "moderate arousal" sweet spot with regard to performance) – but you need to do your best to set aside negative emotions that you may harbor about the outcomes of the process. For the insight-generation process to work effectively, you have to let it lead where it will lead – without judgment. You may or may not decide to act on the results of your insight-generation efforts, but you at least want to let the process run its course to conclusion before making that decision. Just like you need to check your fixed mindset at the door for the insight-generation process to work most effectively, you need to check any emotional baggage (especially fear, denial, guilt and anxiety) at the door as well.

Information Overload and/or Irrelevance

The first three challenges to the insight-generation process – fixed mindsets, functional fixedness and unhelpful emotional states – live squarely within our own heads. By contrast, the fourth challenge – an excess of (potentially irrelevant) information – essentially lives at the intersection of our own minds and the external world. It's the combination of "the tons of stuff that's really out there in the world" and our internal tendency to "boil the ocean" in the search for guidance in our problem-solving efforts.

One of the thorniest factors that can block progress towards insight generation is what I refer to as the "embarrassment of riches" problem. This occurs when you have an excess of information that you're trying to use to find a solution or make a decision – and not all of that information is actually (or equally) useful and relevant. When we're struggling with a problem, one of the most natural tendencies is to try to gather as much information as possible so that we can make an informed decision about the best option available to us. The problem is that if we don't have a way to filter that information – to determine what's most relevant to solving the challenge at hand – we can quickly succumb to a version of "analysis paralysis." Unless all these inputs into our insight-generation process point in the same direction (unlikely, since a problem with such an obvious a solution wouldn't require the insight-generation process in the first place), we can end up unable to make any sort of decision at all.

To combat the drowning-in-data problem, you want to determine which of your inputs are really most relevant to the problem at hand. This may mean weeding out the priorities of people who aren't key stakeholders in the decision (you can't please all the people all the time); information that's outdated or simply irrelevant (not all inputs are created equal); concerns that you have that don't reflect reality (perception is reality – except when it's not); or issues that have relatively little impact in the grand scheme of things (don't sweat the small stuff).

You also have to recognize that as you're trying to solve your central challenge, you're unlikely to be able to maximize all things for all people. For example, when my husband and I were planning our combined honeymoon/one-year-anniversary trip, I just about made myself completely bonkers by trying to craft a trip that maximized seven things simultaneously: romance, adventure, value-for-money, fun, ease-of-execution, relaxation, and general "cool factor." At a certain point I had the epiphany that some of those goals were mutually exclusive, and I was going to have to figure out which of those priorities was most important, otherwise the time for our trip would come and go and I'd still be sitting at my computer trying to run models that maximized everything simultaneously. In my (well-intentioned) desire to make our honeymoon/anniversary holiday The Best Trip Ever, I was actually impeding my progress towards a solution by equally weighting competing priorities in a way that was counterproductive. All data and all priorities are not created equal, so you've got to be able to look at the inputs to your insight-generation efforts and be objective about which ones are mission-critical and which ones you can set aside.

Now, I've use the term "set aside" very specifically here because it alludes to one of the little quirks of the insight-generation process, which is the fact that true insight very often arises from the sudden and unexpected combination of pieces of information that at first seem only distantly related (if at all). Problems that have obvious solutions don't generate moments of insight because the right answer is apparent from the beginning. The light bulb doesn't suddenly come on…because it was never off in the first place. Therefore, it's a bit of a tightrope you have to walk here. You need to focus your attention on those inputs that you think are the most relevant/helpful to your insight-generation efforts – but you don't want to entirely discard the non-obvious/non-central inputs in case they happen to contain the unexpected connections that will lead to that key moment of insight. I admit, it's a little bit like having your cake and eating it too…but there it is.

The best solution I've found for this tightrope walk is to create essentially a "holding pen" for all of the ideas, priorities, inputs – whatever – that you deem non-central to your efforts. And you want to periodically look through all those things to see if they trigger any new connections or ideas as you work your way through the insight-generation process. Sometimes things that seemed tangential at the beginning can turn out to be more critical once you've developed your thinking a bit more, so you don't ever want to throw out any inputs or possibilities entirely – you just want to create a separate space where they can hang out while you work with your primary inputs. In my experience, it's best to create some sort of physical repository for these inputs/ideas, rather than assuming you can simply hold them in your head and remember them whenever you want. So have a separate sheet of paper or box of index cards or computer file that's your "holding pen" and just brain-dump stuff in there. There are no rules for what can go in there – basically, if something occurs to you at any point, it probably does so for a reason, even if you don't know what that reason is at the time, so write it down and store it for later. It doesn't have to be pretty – it just has to be something you can access periodically to see if it sparks any useful connections.

Environmental Blockers

The fifth and final major obstacle to insight-generation efforts completes the transition from internal to external factors by addressing the challenges posed by environmental blockers. These blockers are no less threatening to your efforts than the various internal obstacles were; you just have less control over them and may, therefore, have to be more creative in your search for ways around/over/under/through them.

If you're working on a personal challenge, these environmental blockers are likely to take the form of other people's issues, expectations and preferences trying to impose themselves on you. So, for example, people with fixed mindsets may try to cramp your style as you explore off-the-wall ideas. Or someone else's functional fixedness may limit their ability to see non-obvious options if you ask them for help coming up with creative ideas. Or another person's anxiety about the implications of the insight you're pursuing might prompt them to try to put the brakes on your efforts. Most of these individual-level challenges are addressed with other people in the exact same way you'd address them if they were your own – with the added challenge of having to manage someone else's ego and priorities in the process.

Where there truly *is* a new ripple with regard to environmental blockers is when we're trying to drive to insight in an organization, whether it's a for-profit Fortune 500 company, a community organization, a government institution or any other kind of entity. Some of the most common threats to insight generation that you'll have to address in these organizational settings are: a risk-averse culture, misaligned goals and rewards, and the misuse of rewards and performance evaluation.

Risk-averse cultures are problematic because insight generation so heavily relies on making non-obvious connections between things – and organizations tend to like obvious things much better than non-obvious things. And for colleagues who only see the results of the insight-generation process – without having that "light bulb moment" themselves – your solution or decision can be a tough sell if it's revolutionary or quirky or truly novel. The creation of an organizational culture that's conducive to lots of great stuff – not just the facilitation of insight – is a massive (and massively important) topic that's beyond the scope of this particular book.* However, at the very least, what you should strive to do is create a risk-friendly micro-culture among the people who are working with you on the insight-generation process. To paraphrase Gandhi: Be the change you want to see in the organization.

In addition to the problem of risk-averse cultures, one of the other challenges to insight generation in organizations is the (astoundingly pervasive) problem of misaligned goals and rewards. I'll try to resist the urge to talk about the broader negative effect that this has on pretty much *everything* in organizations and instead restrict my observations to the impact it has on the insight-generation process. The bottom line is that if different people (or teams or divisions or whatever) within the organization have different goals or rewards, it can be very difficult to generate useful moments of insight. At best, you're likely to end up with a series of insights for each of the different stakeholders – and then find yourself struggling to determine how to reconcile all those different solutions. This is not to say that it's impossible to have an insight that is the equivalent of the elusive "Theory of Everything" from the world of science – just that it makes your task more difficult by probably an order of magnitude.

As a result, the first step in addressing this challenge should be to identify all the misaligned goals and rewards that might impact your insight-generation process – and then determine what you can realistically do to reduce, eliminate or make irrelevant those conflicts. This could mean everything from making actual changes such that the conflicts no longer exist (or are minimized), to simply acknowledging the conflicts, to deciding that you need to reframe your problem statement in a way that focuses your efforts on areas with fewer inherent conflicts.

---

* If you're interested in learning more about what makes for a great company culture (and great company performance), be sure to check out the book *Culture Trumps Everything: The Unexpected Truth about the Ways Environment Changes Biology, Psychology, and Behavior* by Dr. Gustavo Grodnitzky.[9] Yep, that Gustavo. It is – even accounting for my own personal bias – super cool.

Unfortunately, the consequences of misaligned rewards aren't the only issues that rewards can cause in the insight-generation process. There's evidence that the mere prospect of rewards – or even just performance evaluation – diminishes performance on insight generation and creative tasks in general.[10]

Research indicates that (perhaps not surprisingly) the prospect of a reward leads people to focus all of their attention on whatever they believe will most likely lead to the reward. Unfortunately, this in turn leads to "an overly explicit mode of processing."[11] Explicit processing means that we're thinking in a structured, logical, rule-based and generally very targeted and precise way. This is great for some things, but it's often the enemy of insight because insight generally resides in the connections between distantly related concepts that explicit, rule-based processing is unlikely to surface.

We see a similar problem when we look at performance evaluation, even if rewards aren't part of the equation. In studies using CRA problems, the threat of performance evaluation increased people's functional fixedness on the most obvious (but incorrect) solutions to the problem, thereby preventing them from discovering the correct (but non-obvious) solutions. Essentially, they were so desperate to avoid failure that they got stuck on the dominant response, which their brains figured was statistically their best shot at success, even at the expense of their ability to continue to search for what was actually the correct answer.[12]

What all of this means is that you should beware of introducing anything that smacks of either evaluation or rewards into your insight-generation efforts. What you may intend as "motivation" is likely to backfire and get you only obvious/dominant/incorrect solutions to your problem.

So What?

Very often, the phenomenon of insight seems to have a mind of its own, appearing when we least expect it – and (rather annoyingly) generally not when we most need it. At first glance, there seems to be relatively little that we can do to conjure it up when we could really use its help. What this chapter demonstrates, however, is that part of the reason why insights don't appear as frequently as we'd like is because of a variety of conditions that actively block the development of insight. And by "conditions" I generally mean "us." Without intending to, we are our own worst enemies when it comes to the insight-generation process. Of the five primary blockers of insight – fixed mindsets, functional fixedness, counterproductive emotions, information overload/irrelevance and environmental blockers – the first three (and possibly four) of them live squarely within our own heads. The good news about the fact that we, ourselves, are usually the source of the problem means that it's also within our power to remove these blockers to insight, as summarized below:

1. **Fixed mindsets:** The solution to a fixed mindset (our own or others') begins with a deep understanding of what it means (and looks like and feels like) to have a growth mindset instead. I've provided a high-level overview of these two mindsets in this chapter, and I highly recommend gaining a deeper understanding of them – and especially how to shift towards a growth mindset – by reading Carol Dweck's outstanding book, *Mindset: The New Psychology of Success.*[13] It rocked my world and completely changed how I do almost everything - to include how I approach the process of insight generation.

2. **Functional fixedness:** Tackling the extremely difficult (yet critical) issue of functional fixedness requires a high degree of self-awareness and the ability to step outside your current thought patterns and ask questions like "What incorrect or overly restrictive assumptions am I making here?" "How could I look at this from an entirely different perspective?" "What are the non-obvious alternatives that I should consider?" "Who can I speak with that would see the things I'm missing?" The key is to recognize that if you've gotten to impasse on a challenge, it's highly likely that it's because you're stuck on a dominant (yet incorrect) search strategy and/or way of seeing the problem and its solutions. It won't necessarily feel that way – but trust me, it's almost invariably true. So work on the assumption that

you've got to find some way to break out of this pattern, either by forcing yourself to take alternative perspectives – or, probably more efficiently, by enlisting the assistance of other people who will have radically different viewpoints to offer.

3. **Counterproductive emotions:** In terms of wrangling the Four Horsemen of the Emotional Apocalypse – fear, denial, guilt and anxiety – the first step is admitting that you have a problem with one or more of them. You have to do an honest assessment of whether any of these counterproductive emotions is influencing your framing of the problem, your solution search strategy and/or the answers you're willing to consider. If they are, drag the underlying issue out into the light and work through it so that it's not impeding your ability to progress towards insight. As they say, "Daylight is a great sanitizer." Once you've gotten the issue under control – or at least managed to safely cage it up for the duration – then you can pick up your insight-generation efforts where you left off.

4. **Information overload and/or irrelevance:** The most effective approach to managing the distracting and/or paralyzing effect of information overload/irrelevance in the insight-generation process is two-fold: (1) identify the most high-value inputs and (2) create a holding pen for everything else. Remember that you're walking a bit of a tightrope here. You have to figure out which of your inputs are most likely to help lead to insight and focus your attention on those – while not losing track entirely of inputs that initially seem tangential, but which may later prove to be essential. Remember that the most obvious inputs may not be the correct ones (see "functional fixedness" above). As a result, you'll want to create a physical repository (notebook, computer file, set of index cards, whatever) where the ideas/inputs you're not actively working on can live – and you'll want to refer back to these periodically to see if they spark the unexpected connections that so often lead to insight.

5. **Environmental blockers:** It's only with the final of the key
   impediments to insight – environmental blockers – that we truly
   encounter problems that arise outside ourselves. If you find yourself
   facing a risk-averse culture, misaligned goals/rewards or a situation
   that simply overemphasizes reward and performance evaluation,
   your challenge will be to find a way to neutralize these factors –
   or do a clever end-around them. Even if you can't fix these issues
   permanently or for the entire organization in question (whether it be
   a company or a family or whatever), to the extent that you can create
   a temporary and/or localized environment that takes these blockers
   off the table, you will significantly increase your chances of getting
   to insight.

CHAPTER 4

Eat, Drink and Be Merry:
Create Conditions Conducive to Insight

About a year into our relationship, Gustavo and I decided to move in together, which meant that he and his two cats would be joining me and my two dogs in my house. I lived in the bigger town and had a house more amenable to creating separate "cat zones" and "dog zones," so we decided that my house would be the better option for a combined household.

As part of my preparation for the arrival of Gustavo and the cats, I went to great lengths to find just the right pet gates to install at the top and bottom of the stairs that connected the first and second floors of the house. The plan was for the dogs to live downstairs, where they had access to my makeshift office and – most importantly – the fenced-in yard. The kitties would live upstairs, where they had access to the bedrooms and Gustavo's makeshift office. Gustavo's two cats were about 17 years old at the time – and my two dogs had never had any exposure to cats (and one of them was very fond of chasing – and sometimes catching – small animals in the back yard), so we had decided that it was safer all around to keep the dogs and cats separate.

The pet gates that I had purchased were the type that actually get secured to the wall/staircase using screws rather than relying just on tension to keep them in place (safety first!). Being a chronic overachiever, I wanted to install them on my own, prior to the arrival of the kitties, so that the dogs would have a chance to acclimate to the new order of things (read: not sleeping on top of me in bed every night). So I whipped out my tools, read the instructions and proceeded to install one gate at the bottom of the stairs and the second gate at the top of the stairs – essentially creating what we referred to as an "airlock" or "the DMZ," meaning that even if a cat or a dog managed to get past one gate, there would still be another gate as a second line of defense.

After a couple of weeks, Gustavo and I noticed that the attachment points on one side of the upper gate seemed to be coming loose from the wall and wobbling around a bit, rather than providing the rock-solid feel we were looking for. This made absolutely no sense to me, since all the other attachment points – on this gate and the gate at the bottom of the stairs – were completely secure, and I'd installed the gates myself following the instructions to the letter, using a stud finder to make sure I was installing the screws directly into the wall studs.

Looking at the wobbly attachment point, Gustavo made the very reasonable observation that, "It's not in the stud." I looked at him and said (somewhat indignantly, I'm afraid), "Yes, it IS in the stud. I know how to use a stud finder." This went back-and-forth for some time, with Gustavo pointing at the wobbly attachment and saying that there's no way it could be screwed into the stud if it's that wobbly. And me saying that I was perfectly capable of using a stud finder and that I was 100% sure that I'd screwed it into the wall precisely where the stud finder indicated the stud was.

After a couple of minutes of this, with each of us firmly holding to our belief, we finally decided to unscrew the gate from the wall. As we pulled the screw out of the wall, we looked at the length of the screw and both instantly realized exactly what the problem was. The screw was perfectly positioned over the stud (as I had claimed), but it was *too short* to reach the stud, so it had been trying to support the gate just in the drywall (as Gustavo had claimed). In all of our back-and-forth discussion about whether the screw was in the right place or not, it never occurred to us that the problem wasn't the *location* of the screw – it was the *length* of the screw. But the moment we pulled the screw out of the wall and saw how short it was, we realized the truth in an instant, which was a possibility that – literally just nanoseconds before – we hadn't even been able to imagine. But the screw came out, the light bulb came on and – click! – we had the solution to our mystery of whether or not it was "in the stud." It was very much a lesson in the dangers of getting so fixated on a finite set of options that you blind yourself to other (potentially more accurate) possibilities.

In a Nutshell

A quick reminder that this chapter and the previous one are like two sides of the same coin, and together they set the stage for success in the Impasse to Insight Method. The previous chapter discussed how you must *take away* the things that *prevent* the attainment of insight; by contrast, this chapter investigates the things that you need to *add* in order to *facilitate* insight. Think of it like setting the table for dinner in a restaurant. First you have to clear away everything left over from the previous meal; then you have to set the table with everything that you'll need for the next meal. Both actions contribute to creating the right conditions for a great meal – one set of behaviors by removing things and the other set of behaviors by adding things.*

There are five major factors that you can add to your insight-generation efforts that will help facilitate insight, and they range from the somewhat philosophical to the intensely tactical. In order from most philosophical to most tactical, they are: (1) be open to alternative solutions, (2) be in

---

* Although there are individual factors that we have no conscious control over that impact our individual insight-generation abilities (for example, IQ), my focus in this chapter will be on those factors that we can consciously control. As interesting as it may be to learn that people who score higher on standard IQ tests also perform better on insight problems in the lab,[1] I'm not sure what you do with that information in a practical sense. IQ is pretty stable by the time we reach adulthood, so knowing that hey, it would be nice to have more of it so I could be better at solving problems via insight is all well and good – but I can't really do anything about it.

the correct frame of mind, (3) seek out diverse collaborators, (4) work during your non-optimal times of day and (5) make it a point to go to happy hour.

Be Open to Alternative Solutions

Certainty is the enemy of insight. One of the most important skillsets required for effective insight generation is the ability to handle ambiguity. The method requires you to remain open to all alternatives – no matter how undesirable or seemingly unlikely they may be – right up until the moment when you have that genuine experience of blinding clarity about "The Truth." It's critically important that you don't get attached to individual options, solutions or decisions too early in the process, because it can blind you to other (potentially better) ones as a result. Keep your options open as long as possible.

You also want to be extremely careful about trying to "reverse-engineer" the process. Very often we know where we *want* to end up, and so at each step in the process we're not allowing it to play out as it should; instead we're the invisible force behind the curtain, attempting to guide the outcomes like the Wizard of Oz. There's a saying that "If you can't handle the answer, then you shouldn't ask the question" – and that's very much true for the insight-generation process as well. If you're going to do it, you need to recognize that the only way it works properly is if you are fully committed to the process – and to whatever outcome it may lead you to.

Also bear in mind that you need to be willing to be wrong. A lot. You need to consider a bunch of ideas and discard most of them. You'll go down lots and lots of paths that won't pan out – but each time that happens, you'll learn more about what is and isn't likely to be a productive area of investigation/connection.

One of the key contributors to keeping an open mind and being willing to consider (and often discard) lots of options is the ability to shift quickly and easily among different lines of thinking, as this rapid shifting helps prevent us from getting "stuck" on an incorrect framing of the problem or an unproductive line of inquiry with regard to a possible solution (i.e., functional fixedness). It also helps us to search out and evaluate many more associations between things to see if there might be a combination that fits the bill for the current challenge we're tackling. The ability to rapidly consider, evaluate and discard or retain lots of divergent associations is essential to successful insight generation. Like most skills and abilities, there is individual variation in terms of how well we each engage in this sort of divergent thinking, which is defined as non-linear, associative and holistic.[2]

The good news is that there are some very simple things that all of us can do to enhance our divergent-thinking abilities as we prepare to tackle a problem or challenge that we think would be well served by an insight solution. Researchers have consistently found that engaging in a specific type of task that encourages creative, divergent thinking subsequently improves people's performance on insight-related problems.[3] The most intuitive of these tasks are variations on what are referred to as the "Alternative Uses Task" (the "AUT") or the "Unusual Uses Task" (the "UUT"). In the Alternative Uses Task (AUT) exercise, people are asked to generate as many alternative uses for a common object (such as a fork) as possible (in the UUT, the instructions are more directive about asking for "unusual" uses). So I might come up with alternative uses such as paperweight, screwdriver, backscratcher, self-defense weapon (in a pinch), tool to retrieve objects that have rolled under the refrigerator – and so on, until I either run out of ideas or run out of time.

What researchers have discovered is that people who engage in AUT tasks immediately before tackling insight problems (including ones much more complicated than the traditional compound remote associates (CRA) ones that researchers often use), consistently outperform people who haven't just engaged in these divergent-thinking tasks. And, as you can see in the graph below (Figure 1), the difference in performance is significant; there is a dramatic increase in insight-problem-solving ability among those people who've just completed an AUT exercise compared to those who have not.

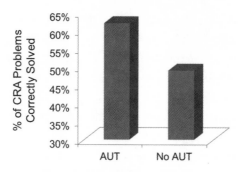

Figure 1: Overall success rate for participants attempting to solve CRA problems either following exposure to an AUT exercise or without exposure to an AUT exercise.

What researchers believe these AUT exercises allow people to do is essentially "grease the gears" of their brain's associative abilities – in more technical terms, this means encouraging their ability to engage in fluid thinking. This belief is borne out by studies that assess the impact of AUT tasks on what's called "fluid intelligence," as measured by the Cattell Culture Fair (CCF) test.[4] This test requires people to consider a series of fourteen problems – each of which includes five abstract shapes or figures – and then to pick "which of these is not like the others."[5]

As you can see in the figure below (Figure 2), exposure to an AUT exercise prior to completing the CCF test significantly improves people's performance on the CCF.

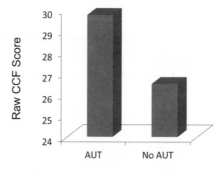

Figure 2: Exposure to an AUT experience increases fluid intelligence as measured by the CCF test.

Eat, Drink and Be Merry

What these results indicate is that completion of an AUT exercise essentially "loosens up" our brains. It is this "loosening up" of our brains – and the corresponding ability to think flexibly about stimuli that are presented to us – that is believed to enhance our insight problem-solving ability as well. Flexible, creative and associative thought is essential to insight generation, and these studies clearly indicate that although there are individual differences in our divergent-thinking abilities, there are very specific – and highly effective – things we can all do to "grease the gears" of our brains and improve our ability to get to insightful solutions to our challenges.

One important thing to note is that the effect of the AUT on our insight-problem-solving abilities is fleeting; generally speaking, the impact fades approximately 45-50 minutes after we've completed the AUT task if we don't do anything to sustain the effect. Bottom line: if you want to give your brain an AUT boost before engaging in your targeted insight-generation efforts, you want to do it immediately before you switch over to your insight efforts, as the benefit will wear off if you don't jump right on it. Think of it like the warm-up you do before an intense workout at the gym; you want to do that warm-up and then immediately dive into your workout, otherwise your muscles cool back down and you lose the benefit.

Find Your Happy Place

The second of the more philosophical enablers of insight has to do with approaching the task in the right frame of mind, as emotions play a significant role in the insight-generation process. On rare occasions you can make "negative" – or at least "stressful" – emotions work to your advantage in subsequent steps of the Impasse to Insight Method. Most of the time, however, positive states of mind are more conducive to insight than negative states of mind (remember that this is especially true for anxiety, one of the Four Horsemen of the Emotional Apocalypse).

When it comes to facilitating people's ability to achieve insight, what researchers find works best is a "positive affect state" (to use the technical term). Basically, you want to be in a good mood, rather than in a bad mood or a neutral mood. Fortunately, it generally only takes a mildly positive mood to get the insight-enhancing effect, so there's no need to try to get yourself to a state of utter bliss (which is good, because if you're struggling with a really challenging problem or situation, your ability to get to "utter bliss" is probably pretty limited).

There are lots of studies that detail the impact of positive mood on insight, and some of the most robust work in the field is being done by the brain researchers and their EEG and fMRI machines. Subramaniam et al.[6] investigated the relationship between mood and problem-solving ability using 135 compound remote associates (CRA) problems and found significant differences in overall success rates when they compared the third of participants with the highest positive mood levels to the third of participants with the lowest positive mood levels. As you can see in the graph below (Figure 3), the high-positive-mood people solved on average 60 CRA problems, whereas the low-positive-mood folks solved on average only 51.3 problems. Given that there wasn't even a very big spread in mood scores between the "high positive mood" group and the "low positive mood" group (i.e., most of their participants were fairly similar in terms of mood states), this is a huge difference in performance.

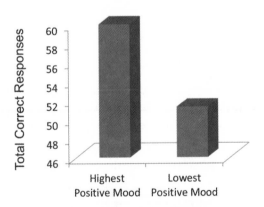

Figure 3: The one-third of participants with the highest positive mood scores solved significantly more CRA problems than the one-third of participants with the lowest positive mood scores.

Eat, Drink and Be Merry

What's particularly interesting about these findings is that the highest-positive-mood people ended up solving more problems overall only because they solved so many more problems via insight than via analytic methods when compared to the lowest-positive-mood people. The graph below (Figure 4) indicates the total number of problems solved (the overall height of the bar), how many of those problems were solved via analytic methods (the bottom, dark-gray-shaded portion of each bar) and via insight (the top, light-gray-shaded portion of each bar).

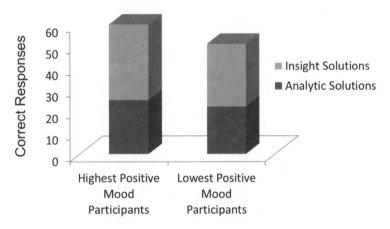

Figure 4: Highest-positive-mood participants solved significantly more CRA problems via insight than did lowest-positive-mood participants.

What you can see is that both groups solved approximately the same number of problems using analytic methods (the bottom part of each bar) – but the highest-positive-mood people solved significantly more problems via insight (the upper part of each bar) than the lowest-positive-mood folks. So again, the overall gains in problem-solving ability among high-positive-mood participants were entirely due to the fact that they were able to solve many more problems via insight.

So we know that people with higher positive mood scores do better at solving problems generally – and that this improvement is almost entirely due to their superior ability to solve problems via insight. The obvious question is…why? What is it about being in a positive mood that enhances our ability to achieve insightful solutions to problems? Subramanian et al.'s[7] review of work in this space found support for a variety of mechanisms, all of which may play some role. Positive mood may cause people to broaden their attention focus – meaning to "see the big picture" rather than getting stuck in the details.[8] It may also help them access distant or unusual associations, which is a core element of insightful problem solving.[9] In addition, positive mood may also facilitate switching between a narrow attention mode and a broad attention mode[10] and/or the ability to select alternative perspectives.[11]

Subramanian et al.'s[12] studies take our understanding of the mechanisms of the mood-insight relationship further by providing us with fMRI data that indicate what was actually happening at the neural level in the brain as people solved (or didn't solve) problems – and as they prepared to do so. The most consistent finding was that positive mood states tended to increase neural activity in a part of the brain called the rostral dorsal anterior cingulate cortex (or rostral dACC). This increase in neural activity – primarily during the period when people were preparing to solve an upcoming problem – was also associated with the likelihood for people to solve problems more via insight than via analytic methods.

The exact mechanism by which increased neural activity in the rostral dACC leads to increased insight abilities isn't entirely clear. As with many things, there are a number of competing theories about how it actually works, most of which revolve around the role that the ACC in general is believed to play in a variety of cognitive control processes. Subramanian et al.[13] indicate that they believe the ACC likely monitors a number of things simultaneously that are critical to insight, to include the detection of multiple associations between things, the management of conflict between competing responses, and the selection and monitoring of various strategies for solving the problem at hand. All of these things help our brains decide when it's appropriate to block additional incoming stimuli (so we can maintain focus on something) versus when it's appropriate to switch our attention from one concept or process to a different one. This delicate balance of being able to focus attention –

but also switch it if our brains hit upon a superior search strategy or solution – is critical for effective insight generation. In essence, positive mood states seem to increase neural activity in parts of the brain that predispose us to solve problems via insight, primarily by facilitating how easily we can switch between dominant (but incorrect) strategies to non-obvious (but correct) alternatives.

The implication of all of this research for those of us who are looking to increase our insightful problem-solving abilities outside of the lab is that it behooves us to "find our happy place" (said with tongue firmly planted in cheek) before we sit down to tackle a problem or challenge. We don't need to get to a state of utter bliss, but ideally we want to be in at least a "mildly good mood" – as opposed to a neutral or negative mood. Happily, research has shown that even if we're glass-half-empty folks by nature, we can employ a variety of strategies to temporarily inflate our mood and get the same effect as people who are happy-go-lucky by nature. Researchers are able to get consistent mood effects by doing simple things like offering subjects a small gift or having them watch funny videos.[14] As a result, we ought to be able to employ these sorts of Jedi mind tricks on ourselves as well, tailoring our approach to whatever our own "feel-good" triggers happen to be. Speaking for myself, I find that a little bit of chocolate is a pretty consistent mood elevator, so for me, that's always a good place to start. For other people it might be listening to music, taking a stroll in the park, engaging in meditation, or watching a couple of Grumpy Cat videos on YouTube. Whatever it is that trips your positive mood trigger, try to engage in it before you sit down to tackle a challenge to increase your odds of being able to arrive at an insightful solution.

Seek Out Diverse Collaborators to Join the Process

Shifting from the more philosophical to the more tactical of the factors that facilitate insight, the third enabler is, to put it simply: get help. Accept that you don't know what you don't know. None of us do. Therefore, it is critically important to enlist people with different perspectives, experiences and knowledge bases to assist you with the insight process. Also recognize that some of these people will possibly (even probably) have better ideas than you do. And this is awesome. Insight very often comes from unexpected or distant combinations of ideas – and so the more extensive and diverse your combination possibilities, the better. Remember that if you've gotten to an impasse by trying to solve the challenge on your own, one of the best ways to overcome that impasse is by adding things to the mix that you couldn't bring to it all by yourself.

I inadvertently got a great refresher lesson in this principle myself as I was working on the title for this chapter. My editor wasn't a huge fan of the original title that I'd proposed and had sent me off to think of something better. One week and eight sheets of college-ruled paper full of ideas and random word associations later, I wasn't any closer to coming up with something that fit the bill. Sitting down to dinner with Gustavo one night, I shared with him my frustration and confessed that I'd totally reached an impasse on the issue; I was completely tapped out of any further ideas. I asked him to help me brainstorm some ideas, gave him a rough sense of the sort of thing I was looking for, and we bandied ideas back and forth for a few minutes. Most of the initial ideas he came up with were ones that I'd already considered and rejected for a variety of reasons, but about 15 minutes into the process – and completely out of nowhere – he said, "Eat, Drink and Be Merry." My first thought was, "OK, I have no idea where that came from or what it has to do with anything" (other than maybe the fact that we were sitting at the dinner table) – and then the next instant I realized that it was absolute genius. As you continue to read through this chapter and discover the additional things that create the conditions that facilitate insight, you'll see why it was such an inspired suggestion (hint: there's alcohol involved).

So, not only did I get an inspired title for this chapter, I got a great reminder of just how powerful it is to have a diverse set of collaborators working with you when you're in need of a brilliant insight. Ideally you want to (unlike me in this case) include these folks before you reach an actual impasse…but better late than never.

Defy Your Body Clock

Continuing the march towards the more tactical factors that facilitate insight is the somewhat surprising recommendation to focus your insight-generation efforts on your body's non-dominant times of day.

It is a well-established principle of biology that we are all subject to our body's individual circadian rhythms, to include the cyclical increase and decrease of biological functions such as body temperature, digestive functions, alertness, and physical performance.[15] Just like our various biological functions have peaks and valleys over the course of the day, so do cognitive functions such as attention, memory, decision making and problem solving.[16] Generally speaking, we perform better (both physically and cognitively) when we're at our peak periods of circadian arousal than when we're not – a finding that has been referred to as the "synchrony effect."[17] People who leap out of bed in the morning, refreshed and energized and ready to face the day, tend to do better on tasks in the morning. By contrast, night owls who don't really hit their stride until the evening tend to do better on tasks late in the day.

There appears, however, to be an "insight exception" to the general synchrony rule, in that some studies have shown that people actually do better on insight-generation tasks during their *non-optimal* time of day, rather than their optimal time of day.[18] To test this theory, researchers assessed participants' peak time of day using a measure called the (very awkwardly named) "Morningness Eveningness Questionnaire" (MEQ).* Participants' analytic and insightful problem-solving proficiency was measured using three classic analytic problems and three classic insight problems (not the typical CRA problems used in many insight experiments). The key question was how well people did on each type of test (analytic or insight), depending on whether they were performing the tasks during their peak times (morning for early birds and evening for

---

* If you're interested in determining your own peak time of day, go online and search for the questionnaire by name and you'll find a variety of websites that include the questionnaire – and scoring method – in full.

night owls) or during their non-peak times (evening for the early birds and morning for the night owls).

As you can see in the graph below (Figure 5), there was relatively little impact of peak or non-peak time of day on the analytic problems. Whether people were solving them during their individual peak times or during their non-peak times, performance was essentially the same. Although in the graph there appears to be a slight advantage during peak periods, the difference was not statistically significant.

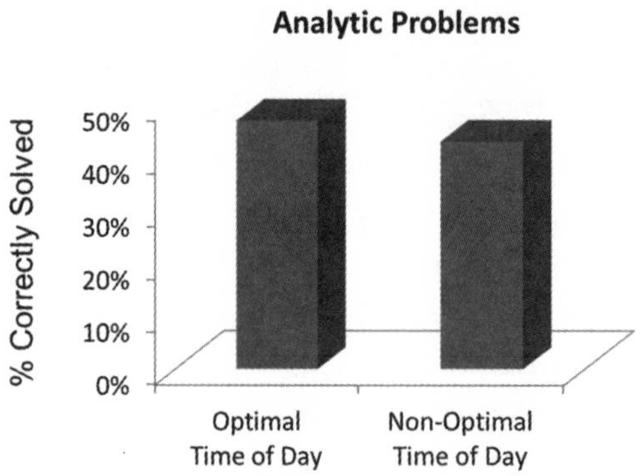

Analytic Problems

Figure 5: Analytic problem-solving proficiency was relatively stable across individual participants' optimal and non-optimal times of day.

However, when we look at the insight problems, we do find a significant difference between performance on those tasks based on time-of-day effects – and what we find is that performance on insight problems is actually better during our *non-optimal* times of day (Figure 6).

Insight Problems

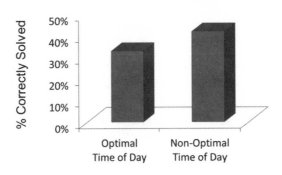

*Figure 6: People are more successful at solving
insight problems during their non-optimal times of day.*

What this means is that the early birds actually did better on insight problems when they tackled them in the evening – and the night owls did better on insight problems when they tackled them in the morning. This flies in the face of the normal synchrony effects we see for most physical and cognitive tasks.

The proposed mechanism underlying this unusual effect is the relationship between inhibitory attentional processing and insight. There is evidence to suggest that inhibitory processing – that is, the brain's ability to keep distracting information from breaking our concentration on something – is particularly affected by time of day and our individual circadian rhythms.[19] During our peak periods (morning for early birds and evening for night owls), we're better able to keep both internal distractions (wayward thoughts) and external distractions (various sensory stimuli) at bay. However, during our non-peak times of day, we're less able to do this, meaning that our minds are more likely to wander to other thoughts and we're more likely to notice sights, sounds, smells and so on around us. Although these distractions are counterproductive to the rigorous, rule-based, intensely-focused attention that's often required for analytic problem solving, they're often just the ticket for insightful problem solving. There's considerable evidence that insight often springs from distant, non-obvious connections between things, so our ability to attend to more diverse inputs (whether internal or external) can work to our advantage. We often reach a state of impasse in our problem-solving efforts because our attention is so narrowly focused on a dominant (but incorrect) strategy or solution that we fail to consider other, non-obvious (but correct) alternatives. During our non-peak times of day, our "mental guard dogs" aren't functioning at their best, meaning that all the distractions that could potentially spark an insight are more likely to break through.

Get a Little Tipsy

The final – and certainly most specific and tactical – of the five insight enablers brings us to the "drink" section of this "Eat, Drink and Be Merry" chapter. For the record, this section is not intended as a license or recommendation to get drunk before doing anything – to include attempting to solve challenging problems via insight. That said, there is evidence that being a little bit tipsy can increase people's ability to achieve insightful solutions to problems, primarily by interfering with people's abilities to concentrate on a single topic and/or by creating a "diffuse attentional state."[20] In many ways, it's hypothesized to be similar to the mechanisms believed to underlie the "non-optimal time of day" effects on insight problem solving.

To test the relationship between intoxication and insightful problem solving, Jarosz and colleagues[21] very carefully and precisely got half of their research subjects moderately drunk using a vodka cranberry drink that had been carefully calibrated based on each individual's body weight.* The target blood alcohol concentration (BAC) was 0.075% —

---

* It should be noted for the record that in this study – as is the case with most other studies involving intentional intoxication of participants – all subjects were (1) of legal drinking age and (2) male, because of concerns about potential unknown pregnancies among female participants. That said, there's no reason to believe that intoxication's impact on insightful problem solving is any different for women than it is for men.

enough that you definitely would not want to be driving (or, say, late-night texting) in that condition. BAC was measured and confirmed prior to beginning the target problem-solving tasks in the study.

The target tasks were the ever-popular CRA (cognitive remote associates) problems, where subjects were given three words (e.g., pine, crab and tree) and asked to come up with one word (apple) that could be combined with each of the three words to make familiar compound words or two-word phrases (pineapple, crabapple and apple tree). After subjects gave their answer to each challenge, they were asked to rate how they solved each problem on a scale of 1 to 7. Numbers towards the low end represented solutions that were achieved more analytically – and numbers towards the high end represented solutions that were achieved more through insight.

The results of the study are surprising on a number of levels. First, the intoxicated subjects solved significantly more CRA problems (58% success rate) than did their sober counterparts (42% success rate). So, despite being quite drunk, subjects in the intoxicated condition really quite massively outperformed their sober colleagues on the most fundamental success factor in the study, which was overall problem solution rate.

The second surprise was that not only did intoxicated subjects solve more problems – they also solved them faster. The mean response time for intoxicated participants was 11.54 seconds (standard deviation of 3.75 seconds) – whereas the mean response time for sober participants was 15.24 seconds (standard deviation of 5.57 seconds).

The underlying reason for both the overall increase in success rate and the decrease in response time is likely the fact that intoxicated subjects solved significantly more problems via insight than did their sober colleagues. In fact, the comparison between the drunk versus sober folks looks almost identical to the comparison between the high-positive-mood versus low-positive-mood folks from earlier in the chapter. If you look at Figure 7 below, you can see the overall success rate for the intoxicated subjects versus the sober subjects, represented by the percentage you see just above each bar.

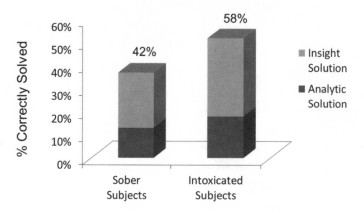

Figure 7: Intoxicated subjects' superior performance on CRA problems overall is almost entirely due to their superior ability to solve these problems via insightful methods.

Within each bar, you can see the relative percentage of solutions that were arrived at via analytic methods (the bottom, dark-gray-shaded portion of each bar) versus the percentage of solutions that were arrived at via insight (the top, light-gray-shaded portion of each bar). What you'll notice is that both groups solved a similar percentage of problems using analytic methods – but the intoxicated subjects solved significantly more problems via insight than did their sober colleagues. As was the case for the high-positive-mood people, virtually all of the "extra" problems that the intoxicated folks solved were ones that they solved via insight. In addition, research has consistently shown that insightful solutions to CRA problems are faster than analytic solutions to CRA problems, and since our drunk folks tended to employ insightful solutions proportionally more often than analytic solutions when contrasted with their sober colleagues, this likely explains their overall faster response times.

How intoxication leads to these effects is – like so many other things – open to some debate. One likely mechanism is that alcohol reduces our brain's so-called "executive functioning," meaning that our ability to control our thoughts, to focus our attention and to apply logic and reasoning are diminished. Generally speaking this probably isn't a good thing – but it might be when it comes to trying to achieve insightful solutions to problems. We know that one of the things that leads to impasse (i.e., the feeling of being mentally "stuck") is fixation on dominant (but incorrect) solutions or problem-solving strategies. To achieve insight, we often need to let go of these more obvious approaches and turn our attention to other options, and a reduction in our ability to hold our concentration on one thing (i.e., fixate on it), might be a contributing factor.

Bottom line: much like I wouldn't suggest eating an entire box of chocolates to elevate your mood prior to engaging in the insight-generation process, I wouldn't necessarily recommend getting drunk either. That said, there does seem to be some evidence that a little bit of alcohol can "grease the gears" of creative problem solving if it reduces your likelihood to fixate on a particular (incorrect) approach or solution.

So What?

Setting yourself up for success in the insight-generation process involves two sides of the same coin: removing factors that block insight (the previous chapter) and adding factors that are conducive to insight (this chapter). Once again, we find that most of the factors in question are under our control, meaning that there are significant steps we can take to both facilitate and accelerate insight. These include being open to alternative solutions, approaching insight-generation in at least a mildly positive mood, seeking out diverse collaborators, tackling insight challenges at our non-optimal times of day and getting a little tipsy.*

The practical implications of each of these factors can be summarized as follows:

1. **Be open to alternative solutions:** Certainty is the enemy of insight. As such, it is critically important to remain open to all possibilities until the moment when you have that genuine flash of insight. If

---

* Unless, of course, this last one is contraindicated in your particular situation for any number of reasons.

you try to reverse-engineer the process towards the outcome you're *hoping* to get, you're unlikely to get to the *truth*, which completely defeats the purpose. Let the insight-generation process lead where it will lead – and then you can decide later whether to act upon the genuine insights you achieve. The choice is always yours.

2. **Find your happy place:** Volumes of research clearly demonstrate that mildly positive moods (as opposed to negative, neutral or wildly euphoric moods) are most conducive to insight. Bearing this in mind, it's wise to either (a) wait until you're in a good headspace to begin your insight-generation efforts or (b) engage in activities that you know will likely elevate your mood and get you to that good headspace. Remember that the bar isn't set impossibly high here; you don't need to get to a state of utter bliss – you just need to get to "mildly positive" in terms of your mood. So before you begin, listen to your favorite music; play with your dog/cat/horse/iguana/whatever; go for a nice walk; watch an episode of your favorite comedy show; or – my personal favorite – have a little bit of chocolate. Do whatever gets you in the mood (so to speak).

3. **Seek out diverse collaborators:** Accept that you don't know what you don't know. As a result, one of the most powerful things you can do to facilitate the insight-generation process is include people who have expertise in areas that represent your own blind spots. Insights very often spring from the unexpected combination of factors that initially seem unrelated, so the more diverse perspectives you can include in your efforts, the more likely you are to discover those distant connections. Remember that if you've gotten to impasse, it's probably because you're fixated on a certain solution-search strategy or a certain way of viewing the situation, so having others offer alternative perspectives is critical. Encourage their participation – and seriously consider what they have to say, even if you don't like it or initially agree with them.

4. **Defy your body clock:** As a general rule, we each perform best when we're operating at our body's optimal time. Early birds tend to

perform most tasks best in the morning, and night owls tend to do better in the evening. Except when it comes to insight generation. When it comes to solving challenges via insight, human beings actually seem to do best when we tackle those types of issues in our non-optimal times. There are a variety of possible explanations for this rather surprising exception to the rule, most of which suggest that during our non-optimal times of day, our minds are prone to wander…often in the direction of the non-obvious connections that our more focused minds didn't consider worthy of attention. So, night owls, this means that you might want to set your alarm extra early on the days you want to tackle insight generation; and early birds, you should grab a cup of coffee and hunker down for a later night than you'd normally prefer. In both cases, don't worry if it feels like you're having a hard time concentrating, since that might be exactly what your mind needs to get you to insight.

5. **Get a little tipsy:** Once again, I feel compelled to include a legal disclaimer that I'm not recommending that you use alcohol in a way that would be illegal, dangerous or unhealthy. Bearing this in mind, there does appear to be evidence that being slightly intoxicated can facilitate insightful problem solving. Much like tackling the task during our non-optimal time of day, mild intoxication is believed to reduce our ability to focus, laser-like, on a single task or idea. Normally this is counterproductive to our efforts, but when it comes to finding and considering non-obvious and/or distant connections between things, it appears to actually be helpful. So, if all else fails, grab a glass of your alcoholic beverage of choice and let Dionysus work his magic on your insight-generation efforts. A designated driver is required for any insight generation that doesn't occur in the safety of your own home (and, please, no late-night texting that you'll regret!).

CHAPTER 5

Ignite the Catalyst:
Deliver a Shock to Your (Belief) System

Earlier in my career I was working for a company that shall remain unnamed, doing research that I found uninspiring and living in a city that I disliked. No, let's be honest, I loathed this city and everything about living there (with the possible exception of some really awesome iced cinnamon buns and a beautiful old music theater). With the benefit of hindsight, there was no question that I was both personally and professionally miserable. But – as my mother has often said to me – "You're not a quitter." For the record, she usually says this with a roll of her eyes in a way that clearly indicates that *any reasonable person* would have quit this crazy situation long ago. And so I continued to plug away at my miserable little existence, trying to suck it up and make the best of it. Because hey, I'm not a quitter.

Then one day one of my colleagues suddenly quit his job for a new job and a new town. At the farewell dinner we threw for him on his final day, he and I were seated next to each other and were chatting about his departure and his excitement regarding his new opportunities. I can't quite remember exactly what led up to this moment, but presumably I was trying – unsuccessfully – to convince him that everything was great in my world. At a certain point he finally asked me in a somewhat exasperated voice, "Yeah, Eve – but are you *happy??*" The question stopped me in my tracks and left me briefly speechless. I paused and thought for a few seconds before finally responding, "I'm not *unhappy*."

My answer still makes me cringe all these years later.

I didn't realize it at the time, but that fateful question – and my unbelievably pathetic and revealing response – set me on the path to a major insight ("My life sucks and I need to radically change everything about it") and to one of the most significant turning points in my life. I had been so wrapped up in merely surviving and trying to get through my day-to-day existence that it took a perspective completely outside of my own head to ask the question that rocked my world and opened my eyes to both the reality of my situation and the full range of possible solutions to my misery.

In a Nutshell

Once the stage for insight has been set by both removing blockers and by creating the conditions that facilitate insight, the next step in the Impasse to Insight Method is to introduce one or more elements that serve as catalysts for the core of the insight-generation process. This is where the magic really begins. Think of it like a chemistry experiment. You've collected all the appropriate ingredients and equipment. You've measured the non-reactive chemicals and put them into the beakers. Now you need to add the spark that sets the reaction in motion. And just like there are highly reactive elements in the world of chemistry, there are catalysts that effectively ignite the insight-generation process as well. In order from the most straightforward to the most sublime, they are: (1) new tools, techniques and information; (2) challenging questions; (3) identification of your breaking point; (4) time pressure; (5) forced choice; (6) unsustainable cognitive dissonance and (7) disconcerting experiences.

New Tools, Techniques and Information

Sometimes we reach an impasse for reasons no more complicated than we simply don't have the knowledge or skills required to solve a particular problem or make a particular decision. If we obtain the new tools/techniques/information we need, then we can generally proceed without further ado.

Although it's probably the most straightforward of the catalysts in theory, it can still be challenging to execute in practice for a couple of reasons. The first is that very often we don't know what we don't know, so it's unclear where we have gaps in our knowledge or skills that we need to fill. When that's the case, our best strategy is generally to seek out some experts in the thing we're struggling with and ask them to help us out.

And, actually, that's also generally the most efficient strategy even when we *do* know where our skill or knowledge gaps are: find an expert and ask for help. The biggest challenge to this approach for most people is having the humility to ask for assistance. Once again, we run into the challenges created by a fixed mindset and the need to "look smart at all times and at all costs." However, if we're going to get the help we need to close the skill or knowledge gaps that are keeping us stuck at an impasse, we have to take a growth mindset approach and shift our focus from "looking smart" to "maximizing learning." And part of that shift involves setting aside our ego and acknowledging (to ourselves and others) that we're not omniscient and/or omnipotent. Remember that the goal is to break through the impasse and get to insight, so you want to view asking for assistance and/or going out there and getting whatever skills and knowledge you need as simply a very effective means to an end, rather than as some sort of deficiency or failure on your part.

Challenging Questions

The previous chapter introduced the idea of seeking out diverse collaborators to facilitate the insight-generation process. Here I expand upon that idea by addressing one of the most powerful things that these diverse collaborators can do for you – whether they do so intentionally or unintentionally. And that is to pose what I refer to as "orthogonal questions." "Orthogonal" means "at a right angle." If you think about a capital letter T, the two lines that make up the T are orthogonal to each other – where they join, they form a right angle (also known as a 90-degree angle). You could also say they're perpendicular to each other in that one goes directly left-and-right and the other goes directly up-and-down.

In the insight-generation process, the idea of an "orthogonal question" is that it forces you to look at the problem – or the possible solutions – from a completely different angle. We're not talking about a slightly different perspective on the issue – we're talking about a perspective that comes completely out of left field and slaps you upside the head with a radically different take on the issue at hand. In the story that begins this chapter, when my departing colleague asked me, "Yeah, Eve – but are you *happy?*" – that was most definitely an orthogonal question. I hadn't been thinking about my life in terms of happy or unhappy – I'd just been stuck in the weeds of trying to make it through every day as best I could. His question snapped me out of my mental rut and made me look at my situation in an entirely new light.

In general, orthogonal questions can serve two distinct purposes in the insight-generation process: (1) they can open up a whole new set of solution possibilities that you hadn't previously considered and/ or (2) they can cause you to reframe the actual problem itself (which, needless to say, would delight the Gestalt psychologists, who believe that "reframing the problem" actually *is* insight).

Do not underestimate the power of orthogonal questions. In my interviews with people for this book – and certainly in my own personal experience as well – powerful and unexpected questions were the catalyst for insights at a disproportionately high rate. Fortunately, there are a number of strategies that you can pursue to generate these types of questions, whether you're working alone or with others.

The most obvious way to ensure orthogonal questions in the insight-generation process is to invite diverse collaborators to work with you (and encourage their active participation), as discussed in the previous chapter. But what if you're working alone, either by choice or by necessity? What can you do to generate orthogonal questions under those conditions?

As it turns out, quite a few things.

You can ask yourself: "If this were someone else's problem I were working on, rather than my own, what tough questions would I ask?" Or you can take the perspective of a particular friend or colleague who you know has smart ideas and/or thinks very differently than you do. So, for example: "What would Mark ask me about this problem if he were here now?" Or you can simply play devil's advocate with yourself: "OK, just for the sake of argument, let me turn this situation on its head."

Basically, as best you can, you want to try to step out of yourself and look at the situation as objectively as possible – and/or from the perspective of someone who you believe would have a very different take on it. Functional fixedness can initially make it difficult to step out of your typical way of seeing the situation – but, like anything, it gets easier with practice.

Identify Your "212"

Not only is it important to identify critical questions in the insight-generation process – it's also important to identify critical tipping points, as these can also accelerate our progress towards insight.

I've been told that there's a rather macabre experiment that's been done involving frogs and boiling water, and it illustrates this point quite well. I don't think I want to know whether anyone has really done this (and please don't do it yourself to test the theory), but regardless, it makes for a great metaphor for this particular insight-generating catalyst.

As the story goes, if you drop a live frog into a pot of boiling water, it will instantly recognize the water as deadly and jump out, thereby saving itself.

If, however, you put a live frog into a pot of room-temperature water, it will simply stay there. And if you slowly raise the temperature one degree at a time – all the way to boiling – the change will be so gradual that the frog will never jump out. It will become increasingly miserable, but it will never actually jump out. It will simply stay there until it's slowly cooked to death.

Eeewwww.

It's a macabre thing to think about – but it provides an outstanding metaphor for human nature (hint: we're not that different from frogs). The truth of the matter is that, very often, we find ourselves in miserable situations that only got to be miserable by degrees. If they'd started off miserable, we'd immediately have jumped out of the pot, so to speak. But they didn't start off miserable – they started out good (or at least OK), and they gradually disintegrated over time, but in ways that were often so subtle that we didn't notice them as they were happening. And before you know it, we're boiled frogs. (Don't tell me that you're not thinking about some previous romantic relationships that went sour as you read this.)

One of the most common catalysts for spontaneous insights consistently turns out to be when someone hits their boiling point, metaphorically speaking. They've been struggling and struggling with a problem or with a decision they just can't make – and then suddenly, one final thing happens and it tips them over the edge. They boil. They crack. They snap. And suddenly, the impasse is broken and the insight and its implications come flooding through.

Knowing this, we can accelerate the process of getting to insight by determining what our own "212" is and then using this information to our advantage.* The first step is having a really honest conversation with ourselves about the point at which we'll simply be unable to sustain the current state of affairs. At what point are we going to boil over? What's going to be the straw that breaks the camel's back? What's going to cause us to crack? Pick your metaphor – there are plenty to choose from.

---

* The boiling point of pure water at sea level is 212 degrees Fahrenheit.

Ignite the Catalyst

Once you've identified the 212 for your current challenge or impasse, then you need to objectively consider how likely it is that this 212-causing situation will to come to fruition. Is it highly likely? Is it only a matter of time? How much time? If your honest assessment of the reality of the situation is: "You know what, this is where the situation is going; it's only a matter of time," then you've got yourself a potentially very powerful catalyst. If you've been holding on to the hope that things will change or improve or be-fixed-by-magic-fairies for a long time, it can be tough to accept that the most likely outcome isn't the one you've hoped for. But if that's the reality, you can save yourself a lot of additional pain and suffering by acknowledging the likely endpoint – and then using that information to accelerate a resolution that allows you to move forward. Basically, engaging in the 212 exercise allows us to skip to the end – to the part where we realize we need to jump out of the pot and save ourselves.

Time Pressure

In addition to saving ourselves time by engaging in the 212 exercise and essentially "skipping to the end" – we can use time to our advantage in another way as well.

There's a saying that "the task expands to fit the time available." What this means is that we often drag out problems or decisions longer than their actual difficulty warrants. If we have a week to make a decision, it takes a week. If we only have five minutes to make that decision, it takes…five minutes. Sometimes we procrastinate because we want to avoid something difficult or unpleasant. Or we get paralyzed because we're afraid to make the wrong decision. Or we think we need just one more piece of data (and one more…and one more…). And sometimes – let's face it – we're just lazy. Whatever the case, if we feel we have infinite time to solve a problem or make a decision…it often takes us an infinite amount of time to get there. But the reality is that most of the time we really *don't* have all of eternity to do things, so we've got to find a way to speed up the process.

Bearing all these very human (and very common) foibles in mind, it's amazing what a little time pressure – whether it's real or manufactured – can do to kick-start the insight-generation process. This is particularly true for "Moment of Reckoning" situations where the insight you're searching for is which of several (usually relatively well-defined) options to choose. If you've delayed making a decision on something for too long, there's huge value to putting a stake in the ground with regard to a decision deadline. You might say, "Tomorrow at noon we're going to have a decision, even if we have to flip a coin" (note: it rarely comes to that). Or, "We're going to limit ourselves to looking at one more research study and then we're going make a decision." Or, "Before my call with Catherine next week I'm going to get my recommendation totally nailed down."

Bear in mind that the time pressure catalyst only works if you hold yourself to it. Working with your brain is like dealing with a small child – if you make threats that you don't follow through on ("Ha, ha! Mom let me stay up late even though I didn't finish my homework!") then it figures out very quickly that you're not serious. The time pressure you create has to be real for it to serve as an effective catalyst. Set a deadline and *stick to it.*[*]

Forced Choice

Just like applying time pressure can help accelerate insights, if you're facing a decision where you're wavering back-and-forth between a limited number of reasonably well-defined options, then playing the forced choice game can help you determine if you do, in fact, have an underlying preference that you're just having trouble accessing (or

---

[*] The story of the Crabapple Incident in the Preface of this book includes a very clear example of the power of time pressure to accelerate insights. Standing at the top of the intermediate ski run with heavy snow falling and the sun setting, I had an extremely limited amount of time to make a decision before I faced the very real prospect of dying from exposure on the mountain overnight. Nothing quite like the threat of impending hypothermia to ignite the insight-generation process.

accepting). Very often, although it feels like we genuinely can't decide between options A, B and C because there's no clear winner...there really is one option that we know is superior. The challenge is just being able to drive that awareness to the surface so that we can recognize (and accept) it.

One variation on the forced choice game that I personally use all the time is simply to flip a coin – but note that you don't actually make your ultimate choice based on the outcome of the coin flip. That's placing way too much faith in chance for my taste. Instead, what you do is flip the coin and then reflect on how you feel about the results. Are you happy with the outcome...or do you think to yourself, "Ummmm...how about two out of three?" Either way, you now know which way you're leaning in terms of your options and can move forward with making your actual (coin-flip-*informed*, not coin-flip-*determined*) choice.

Another way to play the forced choice game is to ask, "If I had to decide *right now*, what would I choose?" It can be excruciating to choose when you feel you're not ready or don't have enough information – but it can also be illuminating in terms of underlying indicators you weren't aware of until you put some decision pressure on yourself. Just like with the coin flip variation, you don't have to hold yourself to the outcome of the "If I had to decide right now" game – but pay attention to the preferences it drives to the surface and use those to inform your ultimate decision.

Leverage Cognitive Dissonance

With the introduction of cognitive dissonance[1] into the set of insight catalysts at our disposal, we've truly begun to shift from the straightforward to the sublime.

In the spirit of full disclosure, I should mention that I think that the concept of cognitive dissonance is one of the coolest things to come out of social psychology...pretty much ever. It's just so darn true. And once you know what it is, you start to see it everywhere – and realize what an incredibly powerful motivator it is.

Simply stated, cognitive dissonance is the (often extreme) emotional distress that results when human beings try to hold two contradictory ideas or beliefs in their heads at the same time. For example:

"I love my boyfriend" + "Our relationship makes me miserable"

"Being a CEO is the best job in the world" + "I'm on the verge of a stress-related heart attack"

"I paid a fortune for my dream car" + "This car totally sucks"

The emotional discomfort that accompanies cognitive dissonance can be a powerful catalyst for the insight-generation process because we as human beings are massively motivated to resolve the dissonance and thereby eliminate the psychological discomfort. So tapping into cognitive dissonance is like awakening the sleeping giant – because once it's awake, it's an extremely powerful force.

To use the power of the sleeping giant to your advantage in the insight-generation process, you need to identify where there are conflicts in your current challenge or impasse. The key is learning how to pull up from the details of a situation and look at the bigger picture. Where do conflicts exist? What is causing me psychological discomfort here? What things are set at cross-purposes to each other?

The goal is to be able to identify the two (or more) conflicting ideas/beliefs/behaviors at play in your current challenge, as it is often *because* you're stuck between these competing issues that you're mired in an impasse in the first place. And to break out of that impasse, one of these things is going to have to give way.

Once you've identified the various conflicting components, you can then evaluate each one as objectively as possible and determine which one(s) can stay – and which one(s) have to go. If an underlying set of conflicts is at the heart of your impasse, sometimes the mere realization of what those conflicting components are is enough to trigger a moment of insight. Other times, you have to actually eliminate the untrue/unsupported components in order to get to insight. And sometimes even the resolution of the cognitive dissonance doesn't get you all the way to insight itself, but it serves as the catalyst that sets in motion the chain of events that eventually leads you all the way there.

Although we generally tend to think of cognitive dissonance as a bad thing because it causes us so much mental discomfort, in the context of the insight-generation process, it's an incredibly powerful catalyst precisely *because* of the discomfort it generates. It illuminates and crystalizes the conflicts that have often brought us to the point of impasse in the first place – and provides us with the psychological kick in the butt we need to break us out of these mental stalemates.

Disconcerting Experiences

The final of the major insight catalysts has the potential to be both the most sublime…and the most disturbing.

There's nothing quite like being suddenly snapped out of the comfortable, familiar bubble of our day-to-day existence to spark the insight-generation process. For most of us, our lives are fairly routine and predictable – because we've gone to a great deal of trouble to make them so. We tend to wake up, eat, work, play and rest in very similar ways day after day after day. We've spent our lifetimes developing routines that work (reasonably) well for us most of the time, and even if we're not 100% happy with these lives or these routines, we tend to be comfortable in them. For lack of a more flowery phrase, we exist in a rut of behaviors, thoughts and emotions most of the time. In this world of habit that we've worked very hard to create for ourselves, we've developed customary ways of seeing the world, ourselves and others. And most of the time, the world, ourselves and others conform to our expectations of them – or at least well enough that we can convince ourselves that they do.

But, every now and then, something so different or unexpected or disturbing happens that it shatters the mental ruts we've fallen into and causes us to see ourselves, others or the world in an entirely new way.

On the other side of these disconcerting experiences, we're changed. We see things differently and there's no going back. As they say, you can't un-ring a bell.

To unleash the power of disconcerting experiences in the insight-generation process, the most important thing you can do is expose yourself to new environments, situations and people. The more you stay in your predictable, comfortable little bubble of familiar existence, the less likely you are to have an experience that can serve as a catalyst for true insight. What this means is that you have to be willing to be uncomfortable. Mentally uncomfortable, physically uncomfortable, or emotionally uncomfortable – and maybe all three. You have to be willing to try new things and step outside – often way outside – your comfort zone. You have to be willing to try and to fail – because you can't expect to be as awesome at new stuff as you are at your old, familiar stuff. You have to commit to seeing – really seeing – the world, yourself and other people as they are, rather than how you hope or expect them to be.

The rut – or "habit" if we want to use a less loaded term – of our thought patterns and behaviors is often what brings us to a point of impasse in the first place, so the goal is to break yourself out of that rut or habit by exposing yourself to situations that fundamentally challenge the way you perceive the world, yourself and others. It's scary – but it also has the potential to be massively illuminating.[*]

So What?

With the introduction of the catalyst into the Impasse to Insight Method, we begin to truly get to the heart of the insight-generation process; this is

---

[*] Legal disclaimer: I'm not suggesting that you deliberately put yourself in harm's way or anything. Your goal is disconcerting experiences – not potentially deadly ones. That said, the couple of times in my life that I've found myself thinking, "You know, I really could die here…" have generally led to life-changing insights (among them: "Don't do that again"). But you do have to survive the experience to derive the benefit, so please don't go so hog-wild in pursuit of insight that you end up winning yourself a (posthumous) Darwin Award.

where the magic really starts to happen. In every single story of insight that I encountered in my research, whether it was a live interview with someone or a review of a previously published tale of insight, there was always – and I do mean *always* – a specific, identifiable catalyst that set the person on an inexorable path to insight. The match was struck and touched to the end of the fuse…and it was only a matter of time until the insight exploded into consciousness. Sometimes it was nearly instantaneous – and other times it had to burn for a while – but once that catalyst was set in motion, insight was virtually inevitable.

Bearing this in mind, it is absolutely essential that you capitalize on one or more of the insight catalysts described in this chapter. What this means in practical terms depends on which of the catalysts you're in a position to leverage:

1. **New tools, techniques and information:** If the only thing that's keeping you from having an insight about something is the fact that you're missing a relevant skill or piece of information, then your challenge is fairly straightforward: go out there and get it. Find someone who's an expert in whatever that thing is and ask for their help; more often than not, they'll be happy to provide it.

2. **Challenging questions:** The "orthogonal question" – that question that comes out of left field and whacks you upside the head with its completely unique, unexpected and often disturbing implications – is an extremely powerful catalyst for insights. If you do nothing else to try to spark the insight-generation process (though of course you *should*), this is the one thing to do. Ideally, you should ask all of your diverse collaborators to give you their best shot; to ask their toughest, most uncomfortable, most off-the-wall questions about your challenge/problem/impasse. Very often, those questions – and/ or the answers that arise in your mind in response to them – will tilt the world on its axis in a way that sends you hurtling towards insight. Worst-case scenario, if you're stuck working on a challenge all by yourself, you can play the role of devil's advocate and ask yourself all the tough questions that others would ask you if they had the chance.

3. **Identify your 212:** Getting to your breaking point is an extremely effective – if painful – catalyst for insight. However, ideally, you don't want to wait for the water to warm degree by degree until you find yourself boiled to death like the frog in our example. Instead, you want to mentally project yourself, your situation and your options into the future and make a determination about what course of action to take well before you reach your boiling (or breaking) point. To the extent that you can vividly imagine how your current situation is likely to play out as the future unfolds, it can illuminate the optimal course of action for you to take now. Essentially, you should ask yourself, "If I were to take this current situation and fast-forward it to its most logical or likely conclusion, what would that be? And knowing that, does it tell me what the optimal solution to my current impasse is?" Generally speaking, it will.

4. **Time pressure:** It is a truth universally acknowledged that the task expands to fit the time available. This is as true for insight generation as it is for everything else. However, since we generally don't have an infinite amount of time to reach insight on something, one tactic we can use to accelerate the process is to impose real or manufactured time pressure. Set a limit on the amount of additional research or thinking you're going to do on the issue at hand. Give yourself a deadline – and stick to it. Very often, the pressure-cooker of a time limit will significantly advance your progress towards insight. Even if you don't get all the way there in the time you've set yourself, you will certainly have accelerated the process.

5. **Forced choice:** A close cousin of time pressure is forced choice. Like time pressure, it can help to illuminate underlying preferences that you may not realize you have and/or that you're reluctant to admit. You can flip a coin or play the "If I had to choose *right now*" game to illuminate these underlying preferences; and remember that you don't have to hold yourself to your answers (or the coin flip) in the moment. You should, however, pay attention to your reaction to the outcome of these little games, since that's where the critical information about your real preferences often lies.

6. **Leverage cognitive dissonance:** Cognitive dissonance – that awful psychological discomfort that we feel when we try to hold two (or more) conflicting ideas, thoughts or beliefs in our heads – can be a powerful catalyst in our insight-generation efforts. We often reach impasse *because* we're attempting to believe two (or more) mutually exclusive things at the same time, so identifying these conflicts and determining which of them get to stay and which of them have to go can significantly accelerate our progress toward insight. Where there is discomfort, there is often dissonance; and where we can identify the source of dissonance, there is often insight.

7. **Disconcerting experiences:** Human beings – all of us – are creatures of habit. Some more than others, but all of us to varying degrees. And because we have habitual ways of seeing and being in the world, there's nothing quite like a truly disconcerting experience to give us a giant shove towards insight. We often get stuck at impasse because we can't (or won't) see a situation, ourselves, other people or the world differently. By contrast, when we put ourselves in positions that are likely to challenge our beliefs – to really rock them to their core – we massively increase our likelihood of revealing the heretofore hidden truth that we had been seeking. As always, it's important to use your (hopefully best) judgment in terms of how "out there" you want to go in your search for these types of disconcerting experiences. The goal is to challenge yourself, not to get yourself arrested, injured or killed, so please don't do anything that you'll live (or not live…) to regret!

CHAPTER 6

Turn Up the Heat:
Fuel the Chain Reaction That Leads to Insight

Hanging by my hands from the strut of the airplane, my body was flapping in the wind as I dangled below the wing, several thousand feet above the ground. The previous week I'd made my first static-line jump from an airplane – and lived to tell the tale – and here I was about to do it a second time. My first jump had been a success in that I'd hit the landing zone and emerged unscathed – but my instructor told me that I'd come off the strut slightly crooked and grazed the little platform just outside the door with my hip. As a result, I didn't fall straight back from the plane, thereby denying myself the image of the plane pulling up and away from me as I fell. Being an overachieving perfectionist, I decided that I needed to do a second jump, because I knew that I could do a better exit. And so here I was, once again dangling from the bottom of an airplane, about to parachute my way back down to the ground.

As scared as I'd been to jump out of a perfectly good plane the first time, it was double – or triple – the fear the second time. Because the second time I knew exactly what I was getting myself into. I was terrified as I drove to the airport; terrified as I went up in the plane; terrified as I climbed out the door at altitude; and I was terrified now as I hung there, trying desperately not to lose my grip on the strut. The jumpmaster's instructions to me were very clear: once you're hanging from the strut,

I'll count to ten – and when I reach ten, then you let go.

"One…"

"Two…"

"Three…"

[Crap – I'm starting to lose my grip! What am I going to do?!?]

"Four…"

"Five…"

[Oh no! I'm never going to make it to ten! I'm going to fall! I'm going to fall!]

"Six…"

"Seven…"

[Hang on a second. The only thing I'm going to do at the count of ten is let go anyway – so if I can't hold on until ten, so what? Screw it and do a good release now rather than trying to hold on for another arbitrary three counts and having the stupid thing slip out of my hands in a bad way.]

"Eight…"

[Later alligator – I'm outta heeeeeeeeeeeere!!!]

And, off I went, into the wild blue yonder. A perfect (if ever-so-slightly-premature) release and a breathtaking (literally) view of the plane pulling up and away from me as I began to free fall back to earth. A moment later I remembered that I was supposed to count to ten myself as a reminder of when the static line would automatically pull my chute. Figuring that a couple of beats had probably already passed as I began my fall, I started counting out loud with "…three…four…five…" To this day it still makes me laugh that I had the presence of mind to make that counting adjustment in mid-air.

Turn Up the Heat

In a Nutshell

The previous chapter investigated the various ways that you can *set in motion* the core of the insight-generation process. The focus of this chapter is on the behaviors that *foster the ensuing chain reaction* so that it doesn't die out before it brings you to the moment of insight. The catalyst begins the process – but, more often than not, the chain reaction *is* the process. And just as there are a variety of catalysts at your disposal, there are also a number of approaches that you can take to foster the chain reaction that ultimately leads you to insight.

The distinguishing feature of the three key chain reaction factors is how much conscious effort each one requires, ranging from "extremely high" to "medium" to "none at all." The highest degree of conscious effort is required for a process that I refer to as "working the issue." At the midpoint of the conscious effort scale is the need to tap into your intuition. The third factor, requiring essentially no conscious effort at all, is a phenomenon called "incubation." Interestingly, the "extremely high" and "none at all" factors are intertwined, so they are discussed together, following an overview of the stand-alone "medium" factor.

Tap into Your Intuition

Full disclosure: I have an uneasy relationship with anything that is not empirically testable and/or that can't be scientifically measured with precision. Stuff that smacks of the "woo-woo" or the "airy-fairy" generally doesn't carry a whole lot of weight with me. Which makes it particularly notable that I genuinely do believe that intuition can play a meaningful role in the insight-generation process.

Unfortunately, I come to this belief via first-hand experience of ignoring my gut – and living to regret it. Enough times to finally conclude that there's something to this whole intuition thing, even if we can't (yet) define or measure it. I have no idea what our intuition or gut actually "is" in a scientific sense. Is it a part of our subconscious that is able to analyze things in unique ways outside of our conscious awareness? Is it some sort of sixth sense that's as real as our "regular" five senses but that we just haven't figured out how to measure or quantify yet? Maybe there is some sort of Jungian "collective unconscious" that we're each tapped into after all?

Gaah! The scientific geek in me completely gets the heebie-jeebies even just writing that sort of stuff. But regardless of what intuition actually "is," one thing that even I (an empiricist to the core) know is that it's real. Sometimes weird and creepy – but real.

The fact of the matter is that it's amazing how often we know – somewhere deep in the core of our being – what the right answer to a challenge is, even if we struggle to access it or admit it. More often than we're willing to acknowledge, we know what we need to do – we just struggle to accept what our gut is telling us.

By tapping into our intuition, we can access information and preferences that live below our surface consciousness and make choices that are truly in alignment with what we know to be true and/or best for us.

To do this, we often need to take a step back from the facts, from the reasoned arguments and from the data – and try to sense what *feels* right. Stand in front of a mirror, look yourself in the eye and ask yourself, "Which decision will I feel better about as I'm trying to fall asleep tonight? A week from now? A year from now?" Think about which choice you can best live with, even in the dark, lonely hours of the night. Imagine yourself having made Decision A. How do you feel? Now imagine yourself having made Decision B. How do you feel?

I find that projecting your choices into the future – really imagining as vividly as possible what you would feel like having made each decision – is an incredibly helpful way to tap into your subconscious knowledge of what the right choice is for you. Decisions that seem complicated and equivocal in the moment can often become quite clear if you think about their long-term effects rather than focusing on just the here-and-now.

Bear in mind that the answer your intuition gives you may not be the one your conscious mind prefers. If the specific answer that you're

Turn Up the Heat

desperately trying to get conflicts with the one that your little inner voice is insisting is true instead, you'll have to make some hard decisions about which option to pursue. I will tell you from personal experience that I've regretted ignoring my little inner voice a lot more often than I've regretted listening to it. Bottom line: *ignore your intuition at your peril.* Mother Nature gave it to you for a reason, so use it.

Work the Issue

To paraphrase the inventor Thomas Edison, insight "is one percent inspiration…and ninety-nine percent perspiration." Sometimes there's just no substitute for slogging your way through the pros and cons of all your various options when you're faced with a challenge. As difficult and frustrating as it can be, you have to persist where others give up. "Working the issue" means churning through all the alternatives and their consequences in a relentless, systematic way. It's not the glamorous part of the process – but it can be the most critical part. Very often, although the moment of insight feels like an instantaneous flash of illumination, the process that leads to that one, magical moment is slow and methodical and requires enormous amounts of perseverance.

I'm reminded of so many singers and actors who toiled away in obscurity for years or even decades before getting their big break. To all the rest of us they looked like "overnight sensations" – but only because we never saw all the hard work and dedication over time that led to their breakthrough moment. The same thing goes for insight; behind that sudden flash of clarity is often an extended period of thoughtful, systematic "working the issue."

What does this look like in practice? You might revise the problem statement – maybe even several times. You might reconsider the pros and cons of each of your options. You might consult additional people or data sources. You might re-crunch the numbers using different assumptions. You might ask yourself more orthogonal questions as you stand in front of the mirror. And one thing you really should do is step back, take a look at everything you've done to that point and ask yourself, "Is there anything I've missed? Have I closed off any options unnecessarily? Have I left any stone unturned or any options unconsidered? Is there anything I've been avoiding that now needs to be considered?"

Sometimes working the issue will get you to insight on its own; but, even if it doesn't, it sets you up for success via the technique of incubation, the final of the three key chain reaction factors.

Incubation

One particularly distinctive characteristic of this final chain-reaction-fostering element is that it's essentially the exact opposite of the previous "work the issue" element. Like Mother Nature, insight has an interesting sense of irony.

Looking across history, it's astonishing to realize how many great discoveries were made when the person in question was not actively working on the issue at hand. There's our old friend Archimedes and his bath-time discovery of the solution to the golden crown question. And the story of the physicist Isaac Newton having his epiphany about gravity when he got bopped on the head by an apple while sitting under an apple tree (or, if you prefer the less colorful version, when he simply saw an apple fall from a tree). And the story of Friedrich August Kekulé, the scientist who discovered the circular structure of benzene (critical to our understanding of pure and applied chemistry), supposedly by dreaming about the image of a snake biting its own tail. The list goes on and on.

In each case, the person in question had done a massive amount of work and preparation – and then either mentally and/or physically stepped away from the challenge. And, lo and behold, the solution suddenly presented itself to them, almost like a bolt from the blue (or an apple to the head).

Like virtually everything else in the insight space, there's considerable debate about the underlying mechanisms of incubation. In their journal article proposing a unified theory of insight (using what are – hands down

Turn Up the Heat

– the most complex mathematical equations in the history of insight), Sébastien Hélie and Ron Sun very conveniently summarized the main theories of incubation, which fall into six categories: (1) unconscious work; (2) conscious work; (3) recovery from fatigue; (4) forgetting of inappropriate mental sets; (5) remote association; and (6) opportunistic assimilation.[1] Each of these is considered in turn below.

Unconscious Work

These theories trace their origins back to Graham Wallas and his 1926 book, *The Art of Thought*.[2] The first step in his multi-part model of the creative thinking process was essentially "work the issue" – but the second step in his model was actually called "incubation." During this phase, the thinker essentially puts the issue out of her conscious mind and doesn't actively work on it at all; the implication being that the idea gets shifted from the conscious mind to the unconscious mind, the latter of which continues to work on it outside of awareness. Essentially all modern theories of incubation that include an "unconscious work" component follow this same model. You take a break from consciously thinking about the issue/challenge/decision at hand – but your unconscious mind continues to chew on it outside of your awareness.

Part of the value of handing the challenge off to your unconscious is that part of your brain can continue to "work the issue" while you go off and do other things. An additional benefit to having your unconscious do the work at this point is because there is evidence to suggest that the processing capacity of our unconscious mind far exceeds that of our conscious mind. There are only so many things we can process at once in our conscious brains (which is why we're not nearly as good at multi-tasking as we think we are) – but the parallel processing ability of our unconscious brains is nearly unlimited. So by giving a problem or issue over to our unconscious brains (i.e., by actively putting it out of our conscious thinking for a time), we allow our unconscious brain to light up like a Christmas tree as it simultaneously tests neural connections in every direction. As a result, we often hit upon that critical (but non-obvious) connection that our conscious brains would never even have considered (or that, at best, would have taken us ages and ages to think of) – and click! – insight is upon us.

Conscious Work

To be entirely honest, I don't find the "conscious work" theories terribly compelling – perhaps in part because they were postulated largely out of frustration with how difficult it is to empirically test any of the "unconscious work" theories. What they suggest is that your brain actually does continue to consciously work on a problem, even as you engage in other (often mundane) activities. But because your brain switches back-and-forth so quickly between working on the problem and engaging in the other activity, once that wonderful insight springs to mind, you forget that you had actually been working on it all along as you were doing the other thing.[3] Honestly, this seems like a bit of a cop-out – and not actually like incubation at all, since you never really stop consciously working on the problem.

Recovery from Fatigue

Of all the categories of incubation theories, this one is by far the simplest. Essentially, the idea here is that struggling with a hard decision or challenge is really mentally exhausting, and there comes a point when your brain is just too tired to come up with an answer. Taking a break (i.e., incubation) allows your brain to rest, which allows your cognitive processing abilities to get a second wind and come up with the solution as a result. Although it does seem likely that incubation gives your brain a rest, it seems unlikely that this alone would be sufficient to generate insights. If all you needed in order to have an insight was a rested brain, you should be able to achieve that at the beginning of the problem-solving process, before you wear yourself out with all the hard conscious thinking that leads you to need a mental break in the first place. So yes, giving your brain a chance to catch its breath probably is helpful generally – but it's not sufficient on its own to explain the phenomenon of incubation.

Forgetting of Inappropriate Mental Sets

Sometimes as we're working on a problem or struggling with a decision, we make assumptions that unnecessarily limit the solutions we allow ourselves to consider. Basically, we create an "out-of-bounds" area in our heads that's much larger than the actual out-of-bounds area defined by the problem itself. If the solution to our problem lies in the inaccurately large out-of-bounds area that we've defined in our head, the only way to get to the solution is to "forget" our overly restrictive boundary lines – and incubation may be one way to do this. As with recovery from mental fatigue, it seems possible that this phenomenon could contribute to the process of insight generation – but it's unlikely to be sufficient on its own.

Remote Association

I think about remote association theories of incubation as the mental equivalent of "clearing the cache" on your internet browser. The idea here is that we store solutions to problems we've previously encountered in our long-term memory. Whenever we encounter a new problem, our brain's first reaction tends to be to access our stores of solutions to previous problems and see if any of them will fit the bill for this new problem, too. Unfortunately, if our new problem doesn't have an off-the-shelf solution, all those previous solutions simply get in the way of us finding the novel solution to this new problem. Alas, the brain wants to try all the previously successful solutions before it invests in trying to find something totally new. In these models, incubation serves as an opportunity for our brains (in background processing mode) to essentially run through and eliminate all the off-the-shelf solutions, thereby accelerating our ability to shift to the search for entirely new solutions.

Opportunistic Assimilation

Very often, unsolved problems will be filed away in our memory, just waiting to be reactivated – and solved – if the right stimulus comes along. According to opportunistic assimilation theories, incubation is a period in which the brain assimilates (i.e., makes order and sense out of) the various environmental stimuli that are constantly bombarding us. Because these unsolved problems are "primed" in our brains (the nagging sense of an uncompleted task), incubation gives us a chance to pick up on weak signals that may have been overlooked when we were laser focused on the task at hand. It's sort of like the fact that you're more likely to notice and pick up a quarter on the street when you're out for a casual stroll than you are when you're rushing to a meeting that you're already late for.

The Power of 10,000 Black Labs

Among the six theories of incubation summarized by Hélie and Sun[4] that I've just described, ranging from unconscious work through to opportunistic assimilation, I personally find variations on the "unconscious work" idea to be the most compelling both from a phenomenological standpoint and from a research standpoint. There's just more data to support the idea that your brain continues to "work the issue" in the background during incubation – and in ways that are often more likely to lead to insight than your conscious brain could achieve alone. That said, there's no reason why most of the other theories (with the possible exception of the conscious work ones, which I simply can't go for) can't also be contributing factors. They're certainly not incompatible with the "unconscious work" theories, and most of them simply provide specific hypotheses about what sort of unconscious work might be going on during incubation.

The fact of the matter is that if the solution to a problem (or the right choice for a decision) were obvious, you wouldn't need to seek out a moment of insight at all because the way forward would be clear from the beginning. But if we're struggling with a problem or decision,

Turn Up the Heat

it's probably because the right answer is hidden in some unlikely combination of far-flung connections or associations. And when that's the case, our unconscious brains have a lot better chance of finding it than our conscious brains. Our conscious brains are great at a lot of things, but they tend to obsess over what they consider the "most likely" or "most obvious" or "allowable" solutions to things, and we can get so fixated trying to make the high-probability solutions work that we can't even imagine – let alone seriously consider – the non-obvious solutions that lie at the fringe of probability.

By contrast, the unconscious brain is largely unconcerned with what's "likely"; it can test an almost infinite number of improbable connections simultaneously, and without judgment. As a result, when the solution to our challenge lies in the realm of the unexpected, it's our unconscious brains that have the best chance of finding it. I think of it as the difference between having one really determined Bloodhound (your conscious brain) looking for a missing object – versus sending 10,000 Black Labs (your unconscious brain) simultaneously radiating out in all directions looking for that missing object. A single Bloodhound might outperform a single Black Lab if they start with a clear scent to follow – but if the scent trail is weak or non-existent (or even false), I like the chances of the 10,000 Black Labs better than the one Bloodhound (Figure 1).

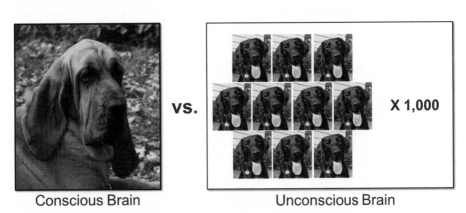

| Conscious Brain | Unconscious Brain |

Figure 1: Comparison of the processing power of the conscious brain versus the unconscious brain.

The beauty of incubation is that even if current research can't tell us with 100% certainty *how* it actually works, what it can tell us is that it does work – and even under *what conditions* it works best. As a result, we can put it to work for us as part of our insight-generation process, even if its inner workings continue to be a mystery (at least for now). Just like we don't need to know the atomic-level chemistry of an internal combustion engine to be able to drive a car perfectly well, we don't need to know every detail about how incubation works to be able to put it to good use.

Ut Na Sio and Thomas C. Ormerod[5] do a nice job of looking across the entire insight research space and summarizing what truly does work when it comes to incubation and insight. Their meta-analysis includes what amounts to 117 individual experiments across 40+ years, with a total of 3,606 participants – and highlights three critical truths when it comes to incubation and insight: (1) the incubation effect is real (i.e., incubation does facilitate insight); (2) incubation is most likely to lead to insight if it follows a long preparation period of actively/consciously working on the problem; and (3) very often, an incubation period that includes "low cognitive load" activities is most likely to facilitate insight (compared to "high cognitive load" activities or no activities whatsoever).

The Incubation Effect Is Real

Across the 117 experiments they analyzed, 85 of them (or 73%) reported positive effect sizes – meaning that the vast majority of experiments found that yes, incubation did lead to increased insights. Across these studies there was enormous variation in experimental methods and underlying hypotheses – but the bottom line is that most experiments did find a significant link between incubation and insight. It should be noted that each of these experiments tended to test a specific condition under which incubation might or might not lead to the facilitation of insight, so most of the experiments that didn't show a link between the two were simply those where the specific incubation conditions weren't optimal. Bottom line: incubation works – and it works best and most reliably under a certain set of conditions.

Incubation and a Long Preparation Period

One of the critical conditions under which incubation works best is if it follows a long and intense period of "working the issue." Basically, if you want incubation to work, you've got to meet it halfway. And, actually, you've probably got to meet it a lot more than halfway. The longer and harder you consciously work to solve a problem, the more likely incubation is to get you the rest of the way to insight. What this means is that you can't just play around with a problem in a casual sort of way, then stop working on it and hope that your unconscious brain with do all the rest of the heavy lifting for you. Alas, all the studies (and, frankly, common sense) clearly indicate that it doesn't work this way. Ideally, you want to work the issue until you hit a true impasse – where you simply cannot go any further – then set the problem aside to incubate.

"Low Cognitive Load" Activities During the Incubation Period

The third consistent finding from Sio and Ormerod's meta-analysis was the fact that what you do during the incubation period has a significant effect on that period's likelihood to lead you to insight.[6] What they found is that occupying yourself with "low cognitive load" activities (i.e., stuff that engages your brain a little bit – but that isn't hugely mentally taxing) is much more likely to lead you to insight than is occupying yourself with "high cognitive load" activities (i.e., stuff that requires all your mental resources). Somewhat surprisingly, they found that "low cognitive load" activities also outperformed "doing nothing" when it came to insight generation. It's a classic Goldilocks story – if you want to maximize the likelihood that a period of incubation will ultimately lead to insight, you want to engage your brain in other activities – but just a bit. Too much or too little and your chances of achieving insight plummet quite dramatically.

Perhaps not surprisingly, this Goldilocks cognitive load data nicely dovetails with many of the classic stories of insight arrived at during periods of incubation (e.g., Archimedes and Newton) – and probably explains why so many of us have insights during a run or in the shower, when our brains are partially engaged in the task at hand, but are largely free to wander. In fact, there's research that looks specifically at the relationship between mind-wandering and creative incubation,[7] and it also finds that incubation most often leads to insights when that incubation time is filled with "low cognitive load" activities that allow the mind to wander optimally.

If we want to take this line of thinking to its logical conclusion, we even find that sleep can facilitate creative problem-solving under certain conditions (also think back to Kekulé and his dream about the snake biting its tail). What researchers have recently found[8] is that people who are working on a difficult problem – and who are allowed to "sleep on it" – solve more problems than people who work on the problem straight through or people who just take a break (but stay awake during the break). The theory here is that REM sleep is very much like putting your brain to work on a "low cognitive load" task – it's engaged a bit, but not to the point of being so massively overburdened that it can't do a whole lot of very useful processing in the background at the same time.

So What?

Sometimes catalysts can be so powerful and so clear that they lead immediately to insight. Very often, however, those catalysts begin a chain reaction that must be fostered and encouraged if it's to ultimately lead to insight. Three key factors can encourage that chain reaction, each of which requires a different investment of cognitive effort on your part, ranging from extremely high ("work the issue"), through medium ("tap into your intuition"), and all the way down to none ("incubation"):

1. **Tap into your intuition:** If you're a highly rational data nerd like I am, you may be tempted to dismiss the role that intuition can play in the insight-generation process. I speak from experience when I say that *you do this at your peril.* You have that little inner voice for

a reason, so quiet your mind and listen for it – then do what it tells you to do.*

2. **Work the issue:** There's simply no substitute for hard work and dedication and pushing yourself until you either reach: (a) insight or (b) impasse. One of the most critical things you can do to encourage insight is to consider the issue at hand from every angle – especially the non-obvious angles. So revisit your problem statement and see if it needs adjusting; ask yourself more orthogonal questions; find some new thought partners who can shine a light on options you may have overlooked; and step back from the details of the issue and see if there are any big-picture considerations you haven't yet investigated. Even if all this work doesn't get you to insight, it will at least get you to a genuine impasse – which, as it turns out, is precisely the condition you need to achieve in order for the final chain reaction factor – incubation – to work.

3. **Incubation:** If you want to maximize the likelihood that your efforts to capitalize on incubation will, in fact, lead you to insight, there are three critical things you'll want to do:

   - **Impasse:** Ideally, you must have "worked the issue" to the point where you have reached a *complete-and-utter impasse*. To use a marathon running analogy, you have to "hit the wall" – meaning that you've got to get to the point where it is impossible to go any further. Research consistently indicates that the more work you put into the problem before you engage in a period of incubation, the more likely it is that this incubation period will to lead to insight. Real-life stories of incubation support this finding as well; you have to advance the ball as much as you possibly can with your conscious mind before turning it over to your unconscious mind to help you over the goal line.

---

* Not to state the obvious, but you should only listen to the little voice inside your head if it's *your* little voice talking to you. If it's some other voice telling you to do crazy, violent or otherwise harmful things, don't listen to it or do what it tells you to do. Get mental health help ASAP.

- **Goldilocks mental engagement during incubation:** Ideally, you want your incubation period to be comprised of activities that require you to engage your brain a little – but not too much or too little. Remember that "low cognitive load" activities are most likely to facilitate insight during incubation. Your brain can't be completely turned off, but it also can't be so busy with a mentally draining task that even your unconscious brain doesn't have time for anything else. Go do something that takes your conscious mind off the target challenge and engages it in unrelated "thinking lite" activities.

- **Sleep on it:** When all else fails, get a little shut-eye. Take an afternoon nap or set the problem aside for the night – ideally after you've worked the issue to genuine impasse. REM (i.e., dreaming) sleep mimics conscious "low cognitive load" activities in insight-facilitating ways, so use it to your advantage.

CHAPTER 7

Was Blind but Now I See:
Experience the Moment of Insight

"**O**h my gosh – I can SEE it!"

I can still hear her exclamation of excitement – and see the look of surprise and delight on her face – nearly fifteen years later. Along with the Crabapple Incident that I described in the Preface, it's one of the experiences that set me on the path to writing this book.

At the time, I was interviewing for a job at a cool research and consulting firm. I had primarily been interviewing for a position on the research team, but at some point one of the senior leaders apparently decided that I should interview for a position on the leadership development and public speaking side of the house as well. The woman who would be interviewing me said that part of the interview would be to "just teach me something" – and it was entirely up to me what that "something" would be when we met the following week.

Thinking back to some of the fun and interactive things I'd done with my Psychology 101 students in graduate school, I decided to teach her how to view stereograms, which are those pictures that at first glance just look like random patterns of dots – but when viewed in a particular way, reveal 3D images hidden within them (Figure 1).

*Figure 1: Top image: Stereogram with the image of a shark "hidden" in it.
Bottom image: The shark that's "hidden" in the top stereogram image.*

I came to the interview with a folder full of visual aids and began with an explanation of how the brain actually constructs a 3D image from a two-dimensional picture. I then handed her a stereogram that had some visual aids marked on it to help train her eyes to relax in the way that they needed to in order to view a stereogram image. She held the image up at the appropriate distance from her face and followed my instructions as I gave them to her, step by step. Then, all of a sudden, she gasped and exclaimed, "Oh my gosh – I can SEE it!"

What I hadn't realized (because she didn't tell me until later) was that she'd actually never been able to see stereograms before – and had always felt a bit left out, since they were all the rage at the time. The rush of understanding she had the moment the 3D image came into view for the first time – and the associated flood of excitement and certainty – perfectly encapsulates what it *feels* like to experience a moment of insight. One moment you're utterly in the dark about something – and the next moment it's as if you've flipped a light switch and – click! – everything has become brilliantly illuminated and crystal clear.

In a Nutshell

I would venture to guess that anyone reading this book has had at least one genuine moment of insight in their lives – and probably more than one. If you have, I don't need to explain the experience to you, since you already know exactly what it feels like. The bottom line is this: if you have to ask if you've had a flash of insight, you haven't. Much like love, if you have to ask the question, the answer is no. But if you don't even have to ask the question to know that the answer is yes, then it's the genuine article.

Bear in mind that there are at least three different categories of insight, and each one can "feel" slightly different when you experience it. The classic "Eureka Moment" is the moment when the answer to a problem or the solution to a challenge suddenly presents itself to you in unmistakable form. In an instant you go from feeling utterly clueless – to having total clarity about the solution. The stereogram story at the beginning of this chapter is an example of this type of insight.

The second type of insight arises from the "Moment of Reckoning" experience, where you're faced with a difficult choice and are trying to decide between two or more distinct options. At the moment of insight, the frustration you felt at not being able to make a choice among the options suddenly gives way to clarity around which option represents the best way forward, and the feeling is often one of relief and determination. The Crabapple Incident from the Preface is an example of this type of insight.

The third type of insight is the "Tectonic Shift." These insights are usually not a response to a specific problem or decision; instead, they occur spontaneously in reaction to an unexpected experience or stimulus that comes out of the blue and makes you think about yourself, others or the world in a very different way. The physiological experience can range from the sudden jolt of a "Eureka Moment" to a more diffuse-yet-profound awareness of a change in your perspective – as if the world has tilted on its axis. The "I'm not *unhappy*" story at the beginning of Chapter 5 is an example of this type of insight.

My personal belief – and certainly my experience while researching this book – is that insights come in truly an infinite array of shapes and sizes, all of which are totally cool. There is some debate in the academic literature about how "big" or "profound" an insight has to be to count as a "real" insight – but that perspective has always seemed (at least to me) unnecessarily judgmental and restrictive. Personally, I don't think anyone other than the person experiencing the insight can assign value or significance to the insight. What's earth-shattering for me might be utterly banal to someone else – and vice-versa. And sometimes insights that seem small at the time can evolve into truly life-changing experiences.

To give you a sense of the enormous variation in insights – and their power to transform our lives if we pay attention to them and leverage them – I've devoted the remainder of this chapter to sharing some of the insight stories that I've encountered in the course of my research for this book. I've chosen to focus on stories from "regular folks" (rather than celebrities or sports heroes or politicians) because that's what most of us are – "regular folks." And our stories are no less inspirational or transformative; in many ways, I think they're even more accessible because they often relate to challenges that we all face. I know that I learned something from every story that people were kind enough to share with me, and I hope you find them inspirational as well.

As you read each story, keep an eye out for the various stages of the Impasse to Insight Method. How well-defined was the problem that the person was attempting to tackle? What did they do to remove insight-generation blockers and/or create conditions that were conducive to insight? What was the catalyst for insight in each story? What orthogonal questions set things in motion? What did each person do to foster the chain reaction that led to insight? And what did they do to turn their insights into actual changes in their personal or professional lives?

By looking for the insight-generation patterns in these real-life stories of insight, you can begin to see how – although each insight is unique – there is remarkable consistency in how insight unfolds. And it is this pattern and this consistency that we can leverage to facilitate and accelerate our own insight-generation efforts.

William

Several years ago I was running a tech company that I'd started out in California, and the company wasn't particularly successful. One of my investors was nonetheless very supportive of me personally, and after a couple of years, I received an invitation to go to this gentleman's New Year's Eve party. I realized immediately that this was a very exclusive event, as most of the guests were people in whose companies he was invested. What struck me immediately at this party, though, was the relationship between this investor and all the other businessmen in the room. At least as the investor perceived it, it was clearly: "I am lord and master…and you are my minions."

I'd seen this investor interact with some of his management teams before, and I was painfully familiar with how he'd interacted with me. Basically, my relationship with this investor over the years had been characterized by intermittent bouts of him screaming and yelling at me – and then periods of praise and support. Now, I'm a former military guy. I've had people yell at me a *lot*. I'm able to deal with it and usually able to tell how much of it is hazing and how much of it is real. And I understood that a lot of what was going on with this guy was hazing and theatrics.

At the elite New Year's Eve party, the first person I was introduced to was a guy who was in his late 50's – but who looked like he was in his early 70's. And the investor said to me, "This is one our biggest investments and one of the people we've worked with the longest!" And all I could do was look at him and think, "This is what it looks like to be put through the ringer for the past 20 years." That poor dude – it was horrible! That's when I truly understood what was going on – and that I was intended to become that person.

What I realized at this party was that the investor actually didn't care about my tech company. What he was doing was making a strategic investment in *me*. I was being groomed to become…a minion. I was going through an acid test period to eventually become one of his management team to go in and run various businesses he owned. And the idea was, through a series of investments in my own company, to make me feel a sense of indebtedness to him. I had kind of suspected this for a while, even though it sounded a little far-fetched. And, sure as shit, the person who followed me as CEO at my tech company after I left – who's a friend of mine – is now also leaving the company. And who is he going to go work for? This investor. Now, for this friend of mine, this is a great, great deal. For me, that was not my plan. Financially it would have been great, but my goal isn't to spend my life building this other guy's empire.

Ironically, his intention by inviting me to the party was to show me that I was now part of that inner circle. What it had was exactly the opposite effect – it made it suddenly clear to me that I needed to start planning my exit from the tech company. Seeing the room full of minions at the party and suddenly realizing that this was his planned path for me too, I realized that it was time to go. Onward and upward on the journey to create *my own* empire – not someone else's.

Was Blind but Now I See

Sarah

In my late teens, I did a bit of modeling – mostly because everyone kept telling me that I should. I can still remember the exact moment when I realized that I wasn't going to pursue it as a career. I was getting my hair and makeup done for a shoot, and the photographer walked into the room, took one look at me and barked to the makeup artist: "She looks like a fucking Barbie doll with those fake eyelashes on! Take them off!"

In that instant, I realized that none of these people saw me as a human being. They saw me as an object. And this was not how I wanted to live my life. I wanted to be appreciated for my intelligence and what I could actually *do* – not for what I looked like. I finished that shoot, walked away from modeling and never looked back.

Paulina

When my first husband got arrested for driving while intoxicated, I had to go to a spousal support group. There were so many women in the group who thought it was somehow their fault that their husband was an alcoholic. I was 26 years old and dumbfounded that someone could really believe that it was their fault and somehow their responsibility.

The moment of insight for me was when the session leader told the group: "You don't have to get off the elevator in the basement."

I thought that was incredibly applicable to many situations in life – not just this one. It was a great mantra that I could remind myself of over and over. It allowed me to say, 'Screw it. I've given all I'm *willing* to give." I realized that it didn't always have to be, "I've given *all that I have* to give." To me there is a very big difference. It means that it's OK to say, "I've decided that I've put as much effort toward this thing as I'm willing to." And have that be the end of it and move on. As a result, I'm able to extricate myself from unhealthy situations much more quickly and not become a martyr for everyone else's problems. If you don't want to grab this life preserver I'm throwing you, that's your choice – but you're not going to drown me with you.

Carlos

I have two kids, and one day it just suddenly came to me that I had to be around for them until they were at least 21 years old and able to make it in the world on their own. I had to maximize my capacity to be here – and that meant that I had to stop smoking immediately. Period. I never had another cigarette after that – and my kids are now in their 40's (and I'm still going strong, too!).

Angelique

The insight that has brought me the most sanity relates to my in-laws. For years I did battle with them about *everything*. The tipping point happened the day after my grandfather – who I was incredibly close to – had passed away rather unexpectedly. My mother-in-law was at my house and she said (and I quote because it is seared into my memory): "You grandmother is really lucky that he died. It's way, way better than him leaving her, like my husband did to me."

I had a knife in my hand because I was cutting veggies and I seriously could have stabbed her in her jugular with it – but it dawned on me that there was no point. Anyone who would say something like that when the man hadn't even been put into the ground yet was certifiably insane. My epiphany was that she clearly did not enjoy good mental health, and, therefore, it was an exercise in futility to try to have a rational discussion with her about anything.

Once I accepted the fact that all my in-laws are completely batshit crazy – and always have been and always will be – it made dealing with them so much easier. Thankfully, my husband and I are completely on the same page where his family is concerned. Together, we literally wrote out our boundaries and behavioral expectations as far as his family goes, presented those to them and for 15 years have been steadfast about holding them to those expectations. We are talking about three addicts, a mentally ill 80-year-old and a woman with borderline personality. We had to get serious!

Was Blind but Now I See

Lily

One insight I often think about has to do with my ex-husband. When we first met – literally within the first couple days – we were in a small group meeting at a conference, and I thought it was really cool because he would jump in and finish my sentences. That happened all the time for the first couple months. It wasn't until probably close to the end of our first year together that he jumped in to finish a sentence of mine (yet again) – and I realized that I actually wasn't going to end that sentence the way he ended it for me. So the next time he did it, I thought more closely about what he said – and realized once again that "Nope, I wasn't going to say that." And that's when I had a flash of insight: "He's not finishing my sentences – he's interrupting me." It sounds sort of silly, but it was a profound insight for me, and that's what really began to shift how I saw him and our relationship. Not surprisingly, we're now divorced (thankfully!).

Ellen

When I had this particular flash of insight, I thought to myself, "Why did it take me so long to realize this?"

I was still working as a nurse, and I was caring for an elderly patient who had a fractured femur. The pathologist who ordered her X-ray determined that the fracture was actually the result of a quite serious disease – but he didn't want the burden of telling her himself, so he decided to leave her in the dark and leave it to this woman's regular doctor to tell her in the morning. I was furious – and my own hands were tied because hospital rules prevented me from revealing the real situation to her myself. I was already so upset with the hospital's policies in general that this felt like the last straw for me, and I was on the verge of quitting.

The poor woman was extremely upset and said she didn't know how she'd make it through the night. I did what I could to comfort her, and left my shift feeling absolutely terrible.

Eve Grodnitzky

When I came to work the following day and saw my patient again, she expressed such incredible gratitude for how much I'd helped her the previous night. I was shocked. What to me had felt like failure – to her had been tremendous compassion and support. In that moment, I realized for the first time the power I had as a nurse – and how little it takes to be able to help someone see something in a different way. I realized that my words truly have the power to help. It really changed how I approached nursing, and from that point on, I paid much more attention to my words and how I delivered them. There's no question that it made me a better nurse and benefitted the hundreds – or maybe even thousands – of patients that I cared for after her.

Fred

I had a reasonable degree of success in the military, and then with several high-profile businesses once I left the military. But I was a hard-ass. I really was. And although I didn't realize it initially, it really limited my ability to manage and motivate people. Then, one day on the trading floor of the New York Stock Exchange, a good friend of mine – who was an extremely well-respected leader both in business and in the community – said to me, "Fred, you intimidate people."

I was *floored*. I can still remember standing there and just staring at him, speechless. It really got to me.

Because I really respected this guy and valued his opinion, I gave a lot of thought to what he'd said over the following days, months and years. And what I realized was that I'd always considered business (and perhaps everything else in life) to be a zero-sum game. To quote Vince Lombardi, "Winning isn't everything – it's the *only* thing." So I'd used a variety of tools to ensure that I won. Whether it was intellectual intimidation, or using my positional authority, or putting on my New York attitude, or just being the tallest guy in the room – I'd been using those things to intimidate people into doing what I wanted them to do.

From the moment my friend made his comment, I gave a lot of thought to how I was being perceived – and I started to plan in advance what

Was Blind but Now I See

I wanted to do differently in interactions with people. It completely changed how I interact with people – and, ironically, has led to successes in both my professional and personal lives that I don't believe I would have otherwise achieved.

Specifically, in my professional and leadership roles, I really switched from a command-and-control style to a coaching style. In command-and-control mode, I'd always assumed that if people weren't performing, it was because they simply *wouldn't* do what was necessary. With that mindset, your job as a leader is simply to put the screws to people and force or intimidate or coerce them into doing what you need them to do.

By contrast, the coaching style that I moved to after my moment of insight started by asking *why* people weren't performing. Was it because they didn't know what to do? They didn't know how to do it? Or (as a last resort) they didn't want to do it? And, as it turns out, most of the time it was because they didn't know what to do and/or they just really didn't have the training or the skills to be able to do it. And so my job as a leader was to work with them to enable them to perform – rather than *assuming* they already could perform and only needed sufficient pressure to do it.

One of the other things I realized after I moved away from the hard-ass command-and-control style to the coaching style was that the coaching style was vastly more natural and comfortable for me. All along I had – without realizing it – been playing a role. I'd been behaving in the way that I thought leaders were supposed to behave and that I thought other people expected me to behave. It was only when I stopped acting in those ways that I realized that it really had been "acting" all along. From then on, I felt much more comfortable in my skin – and was also much more successful as a leader.

Nicole

I was recently diagnosed with a condition called a "frozen shoulder." When asked by my orthopedic surgeon how long it had been frozen, I couldn't recall. Maybe a year? I just dealt with it and moved on with life.

Eve Grodnitzky

The look on her face suggested that…well…it was maybe not normal to be able to live with a frozen shoulder for that long.

Shortly thereafter I had to have "shoulder manipulation under anesthesia" which is a rather innocuous-sounding euphemism that belies the incredibly painful procedure to which it's applied. Basically they give you a nerve block in your shoulder, put you to sleep, and then the surgeon makes your shoulder move in all the ways it's *supposed* to – but that it hasn't been *able* to because tissues have now grown together and connected all the muscles and ligaments. The problem is that in order to get these muscles and ligaments to move…they actually have to tear up all the tissues.

When the nerve block wears off, it's the most incredible pain ever. But then they have to send you to physical therapy *the same day* to start the intensive daily PT regimen to make sure that everything moves and doesn't freeze up again. And every day the physical terrorist/therapist makes you lie on your back and she moves and stretches your arm and shoulder and measures the range of motion, trying to increase it every day.

So about the third day in, I'm with my physical therapist, she's firmly moving my arm up above my head where it has not gone in about a year, and then she's measuring the range of motion with some device. As she's holding my arm in that position, she comments to me, "It's improving every day, and I'm not even pushing you to your limit." To which I reply, "Actually, you are." She looks at me in surprise and says, "I'm pushing you to your limit right now?" And I say, "Beyond it." She really looks taken aback and asks, "Are you in any pain right now?" And I say, "Excruciating."

She quickly, gently puts my arm back down and says, "That's crazy. You're just lying there looking completely calm and collected and you're in excruciating pain? How?" To which I say, "That's my job." She just sort of looked at me for a moment, and then said, "No wonder you got into this trouble in the first place."

And that was my moment of insight. I realized that I was actually killing myself – literally – and not telling anyone about it. I was not asking for help, not saying it's impossible, not pushing back, not revealing any vulnerability on my part. I had grown so accustomed to adopting my "the show must go on" attitude about pretty much everything that my body was breaking apart, and I wasn't paying attention to it.

Since I walked out of the PT office that day, I've really changed the way I work and the way that I take care of myself. It's still early days, but I'm making deliberate decisions every single day that are different because of that aha moment of silent, excruciating pain.

Matt

My business start-up eureka moment occurred on a hot and sunny day in Germany. I was having a barbeque party to celebrate not only the unusual phenomenon of a hot and sunny day in Germany, but also a new opportunity I had to work in private equity in Frankfurt. My friends were all due over in a couple of hours, so I went out to the grocery store to pick up sodas, beer, chips and some ice. I managed to find everything at the store except the ice, so I asked the store manager where I could buy some. And he said, "Sorry, you can't buy ice in Germany."

Whaaaaat??? I'd heard rumors about that before, but had never really given it much thought.

So then I went to another location, this time a little bit bigger grocery. And they told me that the only place to buy ice was at the big wholesale market – but only companies could buy ice there, not individuals, so that didn't do me any good. Not wanting to be entirely unhelpful, they suggested I go to McDonald's and ask for ice. Sadly, this didn't seem like a particularly viable option, given the volume of ice I was looking for.

At this point I thought to myself, "Well, I'm already out – I might as well try one more location." So I went to a gas station and asked if they had ice. Nope, no ice there either. Dumbfounded, I asked the woman behind the counter, "Do other people ask for ice?" And she said, "All…The… Time!"

I paused for a second and then asked her, "If I was selling ice, would you buy it from me?" And she replied, "Immediately!"

"Hmmm…," I thought to myself. How fascinating…

So I took that information home, and – having a couple of hours before my party started – I looked up two publically traded ice companies in the United States. And they were both pretty successful. And there was even a Packaged Ice Association.

If you talk to people who were at my party that evening, the only thing I did the whole night – they'll still mention it to me today – was interrogate the Germans about how they bought, made, and/or used ice cubes.

Following that party I said, "You know what – I think I'm going to sell ice cubes to Germans." The next day, I wrote an executive summary on how I was going to do it. I went on to do about eight months of additional research, and then started the business. And today, you can get our ice not only in Germany, but in many neighboring countries as well.

If I had to pinpoint the actual moment of insight – the clear tipping point – it was the woman at the gas station telling me that people ask for ice cubes *all the time*. And what's really awesome is that a year later she was one of my first customers – and is still one of our highest volume locations.

Juliet

When I was 24 years old, I worked in a nursing home. I *loved* my patients and always suspected that the other caretakers weren't looking after them as well as I was. So one night I decided to sneak in and see how the night shift worker was caring for one of my favorite patients. Much to my amazement, the night shift worker was exactly as caring with patients as

Was Blind but Now I See

I was. Sweet and loving and looking after this little old lady like she was her own grandma.

It was at this point that I realized my trust issues were interfering with my life. The problem wasn't everybody else…it was *me*.

A few days later my boss brought me into her office and proceeded to rip me a new asshole for being a bitch to my coworkers. I zoned out and nodded politely…until she said something that I will remember for the rest of my life – and that I now use every day of my life. She said, "You need to put a filter on your mouth. Before you open your mouth, mentally think of a stop sign and review what you're about to say and ask yourself if it's appropriate."

I swear I didn't talk for days because everything that was ready to come out of my mouth was horrible. I realized that I was just a really mean person. Once I realized this, I spent quite a few years getting taken advantage of because I was trying to be nice, and I figured that standing up for myself was mean. So, basically, for a couple of years I totally over-corrected.

I think now in the last few years I've found a balance. I'm happier, I do good deeds to make other people feel good, I stop and smell the roses, and I truly treasure the friendships that I know are legitimate.

I look at life now like a bank account. The more I put into it, the more I get returned to me in interest. I believe in the karma thing, and instead of getting angry I just move on. It works really well for me now – but it has been a hard, hard thing to learn how to do.

Lexi

My aha moment has to do with leaving a relationship that was both verbally and physically very abusive.

All the times he beat me, I would make excuses for his behavior. It was my fault, I deserved it – whatever I had to tell myself to explain it away.

And he would always promise it would not happen again.

Then one day he totally layed out a guy I had feelings for (the man who is now my husband). The fact that he hurt someone I cared for totally set me off.

I looked at myself in the mirror and said, "You love yourself more than you like this man. LEAVE." And so I did. Not only did I free myself to find true love with the man who's now my husband – I probably saved my life.

Francesca

My moment of insight has the potential to completely change my career path as a teacher.

As a student, I was terrible at math. I struggled to understand it and just plain hated it. It was a point of shame for me that I was so bad at it and didn't understand it.

When I was a beginning teacher, I was terrified that my students would challenge my math lessons and revolt against the mindless worksheets based on rote memorization. I didn't know how to teach any other way. I was worried that I would be exposed as a fraud to their parents.

One day I was helping a student in the second grade. She was really struggling to understand regrouping and borrowing. Unfortunately, I didn't know any other way to explain it to her. Watching her get frustrated and feeling helpless myself, I realized that *my* math story would quickly become *hers* if I didn't do something.

I made a commitment right then to (re)learn the math that I didn't get when I was a student. Fortunately, this happened to coincide with sweeping changes in how we teach math. There were lots of professional development workshops, and for the first time I actually understood the math. And perhaps even more importantly, *I realized that I wasn't stupid.* I just needed it presented to me in a different way; a way that focused on understanding the math versus just memorizing how to solve problems.

Was Blind but Now I See

Inspired by the new relationship I was forming with math, I went back to school and eventually got my master's degree in how to teach math. I now present at workshops and no longer feel like a fraud. There's so much more math I would like to learn, but it's a great feeling to be able to hold my own in a "geeky" math conversation with just about anyone!

Best of all, the relationship my students are forming with math is largely a positive one. They are amazed at how easy math is and beg me for harder problems. Students want to be in my class because of my love of math. Parents know it's in their child's best interests to love it, and they see me as a positive ambassador for math.

I plan to eventually leave my teaching job to become a math consultant who helps other teachers let go of their anxiety of math and learn to love it (or at least understand it better!).

Gabrielle

The recent insight that has brought me a tremendous amount of sanity is realizing that sometimes the answer is just "NO!" There is no flex. There is no negotiating. It's just "no" – and I'm OK with that.

The catalyst for this insight was a situation where my business partner and I were negotiating a transaction with a buyer, and we had bent and bent as far as what her demands were...and she was not showing any signs of being able to flex. We really wanted the deal to work out, but it finally reached the point where the buyer asked for something utterly ridiculous.

My business partner was hemming and hawing, and I just looked at the buyer and said, "The answer is NO." She looked like I'd just slapped her in the face and said, "What do you mean, no?"

I replied, "Is it the N or the O that you are struggling with? No is no is no. We are NOT doing that. We have bent on all sorts of others issues, but there will be no bending on this issue."

Needless to say, the deal fell through…and it turned out to be the best thing that ever happened to us.

After this epiphany – that sometimes, the answer is just no, and that's OK – I was able to have more confidence standing my ground in all areas of my life. I know that not everyone will like me or my reactions to situations and I am perfectly A-OK with that. I will never, ever sell out my self-worth to please someone else. Sometimes the answer is just "no" – and I am confident that the person receiving "no" as the answer will get over it. And if not, then that's OK too, because that's their issue, not mine.

Gunter

It was early 2009, and my consulting work had dried up because of the recession – and the work that I'd do later in my career hadn't really gotten off the ground yet. I was having to dip into my savings, which I hate to do. I'm a licensed psychologist, and I was constantly getting stuff in the mail from various companies that ran clinical counseling programs across the state, trying to get me to apply for positions with them. I finally decided that I needed the income, so I interviewed for one of these positions and was hired.

I hated everything about the job from the moment I started.

A big part of the job was documenting each session I had with the various patients that were referred to me so that the company could be reimbursed by the programs that funded it. One of the patients I saw twice was a man who had absolutely no moments of lucidity at all. He didn't know who he was, he didn't know why he was there in the facility – nothing. He would simply look around the room and state whatever he saw in front of him: "Window…chair…desk…doorknob." I tried to work with what he gave me, but the truth of the matter was that there just wasn't any lucidity or awareness to work with at all. And so I documented exactly this on the paperwork after both of our two sessions.

Was Blind but Now I See

Up until this point, the company had marveled at my ability to quickly and accurately document sessions with patients – but this particular paperwork got rejected and sent back to me. I asked my mentor about it – and he proceeded to try to "educate" me about how I needed to complete the paperwork for a patient like this so that the company would get paid for it. I don't know if it met the legal definition for fraud – but it sure sounded like it, and there was absolutely no way I was going to do it. Sitting there, listening to him try to massage an inconvenient truth into a more palatable falsehood, I realized that this company and its policies were utterly incompatible with my own moral and ethical code.

That session with my mentor took place on a Thursday. I already had that Friday off from work – and I came in on Monday and handed in my resignation. It was clear to me that I'd rather work in a gas station, making an honest living, than at this job that would have required me to compromise my integrity. Happily, my new business took off shortly after I left that position, which I'd like to think was karma's way of validating my decision!

So What?

There's not much to summarize in terms of implementation guidance in this chapter compared to the other chapters, since the focus of this chapter is on "experiencing the moment of insight." During that momentary flash of illumination and understanding, your insight is doing pretty much all of the work for you. One thing that I will highlight one final time is the observation that insights come in all sorts of shapes and sizes – all of which are totally cool. Insights don't have to be profound or earth-shattering to have the potential to change our lives, our businesses, our families and our relationships for the better. Welcome the little day-to-day insights into your life just like you welcome the big ones; and remember that insights that seem small in the moment can expand over time. Like so many things in life, it's not how you start…it's how you finish!

CHAPTER 8

Use It or Lose It:
Transform Insights into Action

Early in 2013, I was sitting on my couch, working through some revisions to my Impasse to Insight Method for this book. I was thinking a lot about authenticity and the power that insights have to reveal the true nature of things when – BAM! – I got completely blindsided by an insight of my own: "I've spent the past 15 years of my life as an actress."

Well…shit.

I had a flashback to about eight years ago, when I was asked to help a colleague who was struggling to perform well when he spoke in front of large, formal audiences of senior executives. He consistently got terrific scores in smaller, more intimate and informal meetings – but he was getting hammered at our big conferences.

Working with him, I realized that when he got up to speak in front of the big, high-powered groups, he turned into what I called "Presentation Man." He was no longer his regular, charming, totally engaging self up there; instead, he was acting the part of the stiff and formal presenter that he thought he was supposed to be in those settings. And it was a total train wreck. Once we realized this, our focus became deprogramming him of all of these expectations (real and imagined) and just letting him be his own, wonderful self instead.

Eve Grodnitzky

Sitting on my couch all these years later, I realized that I'd been acting too – I'd just been so good at it that no one had realized that my "Polished Presentation Machine" persona was an act. Not even me.

And so I asked myself who I thought I really was. With my spiral notebook in my lap, I started to write down the words that I felt genuinely described me and my authentic teaching style.

Accessible. Illuminating. Fun. Smart. Casual. Irreverent. Engaging. Honest. Inspiring. Empowering. Challenging. Supportive. Creative. Brave.

As I looked at those words, I realized that the most authentic version of me wasn't "polished presentation machine" – it was "favorite college professor." The teacher whose classes you'd take every semester, no matter what the subject was, because you knew it was going to be totally awesome.

And so, also being a research geek at heart, I decided to try an experiment. I decided to start showing up at all my leadership development sessions around the world just as…me. No more carefully controlled presentation robot. No more stuffy suits and boring (and painful!) shoes. No more formality. Just…me.

And it was awesome. Every single time. For every audience. On every continent.

What I realized is that just like dogs can sense fear, people can sense authenticity – and they respond to it in the most awe-inspiring ways. The fun, casual, inspiring brainiac that's showed up to teach all my sessions since my moment of insight is the real me – and I've decided that she's here to stay.

In a Nutshell

Although experiencing a moment of insight feels like the end of a challenging journey…it's really just the beginning. As electrifying as it can feel to experience that shock of understanding or to suddenly see yourself, others or the world in an entirely new light – it's what happens *after* that initial moment of insight that really matters. Think of it like driving. The insight itself is the gasoline – and the actions you take after you've had your insight represent the car. The insight provides the fuel that gives you the energy to move forward – and the actions you engage in after you've had the insight are the vehicle that the insight is intended to power. Both components are critically important to get you from where you are now to where you want to be instead.

The bottom line is that the true value of insights lies in their implementation; in how they change the ways you think, feel and behave. An insight without implementation is just a great idea – but an insight combined with action has the power to truly transform you.

At the highest level, there are two paths forward once your insight has blazed to life. Well, technically, I suppose there are actually three paths. The shortest and least interesting path is simply to do nothing and let your insight die on the vine. That is always an option, although the stories people told me of ignoring insights were almost invariably stories of regret. If they'd had a do-over, virtually every single one of these folks would have listened to – and acted upon – the insight, rather than ignoring it and hoping it would go away (hint: it won't).

Assuming that you do decide to act upon your insight, you then have two approaches at your disposal, depending on the nature of the insight and its implications for implementation. On the one hand, if the implications of your insight are blatantly obvious *and* if it would be easy and unproblematic to execute on these implications…then off you go. With a nod to Nike, you just go do it. Thinking about the Crabapple Incident from the Preface, when I had the insight that said, essentially, "You can do this" – then the only thing left to do was to…just do it. Voilà – my insight immediately transformed into my new reality as I went schussing down the ski slope.

Alas, not all insights are quite so straightforward in their implementation. You may not know how to translate your insight into reality. Or it may be extremely difficult to translate your insight into reality. Or it might be both. When this is the case (and, honestly, it's going to be the case more often than not), execution is a bit more complicated than "just do it." Fortunately, there are ways to map out a path forward even under these more challenging circumstances. The six key steps in this path are: (1) give voice to your insight; (2) identify the insight preventers and enablers; (3) define your post-insight reality and its importance; (4) identify 1+1 lily pads; (5) rally supporters and neutralize saboteurs; and (6) rinse and repeat.

Give Voice to Your Insight

The first thing you can do to help transform your insight into reality is to give it voice. Literally. Say your insight out loud, just to yourself at first. There's something about saying it – and hearing it spoken – that begins to make what was initially just a thought feel more real, concrete and possible. You can also reassure yourself that acting on your insight is always a choice. You can choose to act on it – or you can choose not to act on it. The choice is always yours. This tends to (quite usefully) reduce the anxiety that mind-blowing insights can initially generate.

After you've said it – out loud – to yourself, tell your insight to one or more people you trust. Ideally, you want to choose people who don't have an agenda of their own and/or who are not likely to be impacted by the implications of your insight, as you want to get feedback and support that is as objective as possible at this point.

I cannot overemphasize the importance of sharing your insight with a small circle of trusted friends/family/colleagues. Telling other people about it makes your insight more real to you – and, assuming you choose wisely, the people you share your insight with can give you the courage to proceed if your own courage fails you. This is critically important early on, especially if there are significant and/or difficult implications of your insight.

Use It or Lose It

Identify the Insight Preventers and Enablers

After you've given voice to your insight – to yourself and to others – the next thing you need to do is essentially an "after action review" on the insight itself. Critically, you want to determine two things: (1) what prevented you from seeing this truth (i.e., having the insight) before; and (2) what allowed you to suddenly see it now.

There are two primary reasons why it's important to understand the conditions that prevented you from having this insight until now. First, shining a light on all the things that previously kept you in the dark can very often reveal additional insights in adjacent areas. Your initial insight may have turned on a single overhead light dangling in the center of a dark basement – and now you want to grab a flashlight and do a full sweep of the room to see if there's anything else hiding in the corners that you need to drag into the light and address.

Second, a deeper understanding of the factors that initially kept you in the dark with regard to this brilliant new insight you've had will help to ensure that you don't slide backwards into your pre-insight state. Generally speaking, once you understand the full extent of your pre-insight ignorance or delusion, there's no going back.

Some of the key questions you should ask yourself are:

- What did I simply fail to see in the situation – and why?

- What did I misinterpret in the situation – and why?

- What did I actively delude myself about in the situation – and why?

- What early warning indicators did I ignore – and why?

- What can I do to ensure that this sort of situation doesn't happen again?

Once you have a thorough understanding of what prevented you from having this insight until now, the next step is to look at the other side of that equation. What actually allowed you to have this insight at this point? Generally speaking, there will have been some sort of change – in you, in the situation or in other people – that allowed things to click into place in ways that they previously hadn't. Understanding what these differences are can help to fuel forward progress by underscoring the fact that the process of change has already begun – and your job is now to take charge of it and direct it towards your desired post-insight reality.

Some of the key questions you should ask yourself are:

- What allowed me to see this reality now, when I couldn't before?

- What changed in the situation that helped things click into place?

- What lessons do I want to take away about how to see things more clearly in the future?

Define Your Post-Insight Reality and Its Importance

Once you've done your post-insight after action review – and determined if there are any additional insights hiding in the corners of your mental basement that need to join your initial insight under the spotlight – it's time to get serious about defining what your post-insight reality would look like, should you decide to pursue it (and remember, it's always a choice).

The first step is to try to imagine – in as much detail as possible – what the reality of your post-insight state would look like if you could bring it to full fruition. What would the good, the bad and the ugly of that future, alternative situation be? How would you think differently, behave differently, feel differently? How would the people around you be different? How would your world and your environment be different? Compare-and-contrast the various elements of your theorized post-insight reality to your current state. What's better? What's worse? What's just…different?

When you look across the full spectrum of pros and cons (and, realistically, there are going to be both), what would be the net effect of actually implementing your post-insight reality? Would your life on balance be better – or would it on balance be worse? If it would be worse, then that's probably where the story ends. If, however, your life would, on balance, be better in this post-insight reality, it's also worth asking yourself how important it is to you to obtain this net increase in your life. If it's not very important to you – then maybe the story still ends here. Maybe it's not worth the effort of making the change if the overall gain is small, or if the improvements are in areas that you just don't care that much about.

More often than not, however, what this analysis will reveal to you is that (a) life would be a lot better if you could make this insight your new reality and (b) the changes for the better are in areas that are very important to you. Generally speaking, we don't have insights about stuff that we don't care about (our brains are too busy working on stuff that we *do* care about) – so if we've had a genuine insight, it's a pretty clear indicator that it's worth turning that insight into reality.

Identify 1+1 Lily Pads

If you've made it this far, you've determined that the post-insight reality that you have defined is both appealing and important to you. Now it's time to map out how to get from here to there. Despite my reluctance to use another frog analogy (at least the frog lives in this one), it really is the best way to think about the task at hand. You're a frog on the near shore of a river (your current reality) and you're trying to get to the far shore of the river (your superior, post-insight reality). And the way to get from this shore to that shore is by hopping from lily pad to lily pad, since it's usually too far to jump all in one shot (and let's also assume that the current is too swift for you just to swim there).

To begin, you want to identify the smallest meaningful step (or hop) you can take that will move you in the direction of your goal (i.e., your post-insight reality) – and a time frame for completion of this first step. So, what's the first – very small – thing that you can do that will set this change in motion?

There are three key reasons why you want to begin with the smallest meaningful step you can: (1) an initial small step will reduce your anxiety about beginning this change; (2) a small step gives you an early, easy win that gives you some momentum to continue; and (3) it acknowledges that permanent change is much more likely to stick if it happens incrementally rather than all at once (which, for example, is one of the many reasons that crash diets don't work).

Once you've identified this first lily pad and the time frame by which you want to have hopped to it, you do the exact same thing for lily pad #2. What would your second small step look like – and what would the time frame for that one be? It is important to note that you map out lily pad #2 *before you actually make the jump to the first lily pad*. So before you even leave the near shore, you've got a game plan – and a time frame – for the first two changes you want to make.

This is a pattern that you will repeat all the way to the other side; you always want to have 1+1 lily pads mapped out in front of you. The reasons for this are twofold. First, by always planning two steps ahead, there's never a moment when you complete one step and don't know what to do next; as a result, you significantly reduce the likelihood that your forward progress will stall out. Second, planning out only two moves ahead (rather than, say, 10 or 20 moves) keeps your options open as you progress across the river and other, alternative lily pads come into view. You don't want to get so fixated on your initial plan that you miss superior options that present themselves as you go along. By planning 1+1 moves ahead, you ensure forward momentum while simultaneously allowing yourself to pick the best options as they present themselves.

Rally Supporters and Neutralize Saboteurs

I am really resisting the urge to say that in order to bring your post-insight reality to fruition, it takes a village.

OK, so I didn't entirely resist the urge. But the truth of the matter is that your new reality *isn't* created in a vacuum – it's created in the context of the world and the relationships that you live in every day. As a result, you want to think very carefully about who can support you in your efforts – and who is likely to thwart them. The implications of this are relatively straightforward. First, you want to surround yourself with the people who are going to be actively supportive of your change efforts. They can provide emotional support, practical support or both. They are people who do not have an agenda, other than to be supportive of you and your efforts. And it is better to have a small team of dedicated supporters than a large team of half-hearted ones.

At the same time that you're surrounding yourself with stalwart supporters, you also want to be neutralizing detractors. What "neutralize" means for any particular individual will depend on the nature of your relationship with that person. Some people might need to be cut out of your life entirely (and, frankly, for those folks the removal is probably long overdue). Possible saboteurs that you can't completely eliminate are, of course, trickier to deal with. Often the best strategy with these folks is to keep your insight journey a secret from them until you're safely on the other shore and then simply present it as a *fait accompli*. If that's not an option, you can share your plan with them and tell them that if they cannot be supportive, you would ask that they at least not actively interfere with your efforts. One way or another, you will want to minimize your interactions with naysayers and maximize your interactions with your support crew.

Rinse and Repeat

The only thing left to you at this point is to make those first two jumps to the lily pads – and then, as they say, "rinse and repeat." Once you accomplish your first small step (and you will), think about the next lily pad you want to add to keep you always looking 1+1 steps ahead. You will do this each time you accomplish a step so that you ensure forward momentum while keeping the steps small and manageable. As you gain confidence and begin to practice elements of your post-insight reality, your steps can get bigger and bolder if you want them to; or you can keep them smaller and more modest. The goal is to make it to the other side, and if slow and steady feels more manageable, then that's exactly what you should do. At some point, whether you're taking big leaps or little ones, you will notice that the pull of the opposite shore (your post-insight reality) is stronger than the pull of what was originally the near shore (your pre-insight reality). When this happens, you'll know that you've crossed the halfway point in your journey. I always think there's something encouraging about that crossover point, because it means that the shortest distance to *any* solid ground is now forward, rather than backward, and this always seems to deliver a second wind when we really need it.

Useful Things to Keep in Mind About Change in General

I would be remiss if I ended this chapter on transforming insights into action if I didn't address the challenges that change in all its various forms presents for us as human beings – and prepare you for how to handle these challenges.

As a species, we have a natural wariness about change, despite its inevitability. This is as true for insight-inspired change as it is for every other type of change. Probably something about our ancestors having to constantly scan the horizon for saber-toothed tigers or other troublesome creatures that could spring out of nowhere and eat us when we least expected it. Whatever the case, it's amazing how often we'll stay in an uncomfortable (or even downright miserable) situation rather than risk an unknown alternative. As the saying goes, "Better the devil you know…than the devil you don't." What's generally at the root of this resistance to change is one of the Four Horsemen from Chapter 3: fear. Or more specifically, fear of loss. As bad as things might be right now, we worry that any change will only make them worse. Out of the frying pan and into the fire, as they say.

And, even leaving aside the fear problem, there's simply the issue of inertia – also known as habit. We don't like to admit it because it doesn't sound very cool or vibrant, but we are creatures of habit in virtually everything we do. Having developed certain ways of thinking, feeling and behaving, we are loath to change them – even when they're not working very well for us. It's a lot easier just to keep doing what we're doing rather than make the effort to shake everything up. Remember your high school physics? An object in motion tends to stay in motion. Same thing with human beings and habits.

One of the most important things we can do to ensure that we're able to bring our post-insight reality to fruition is to realize that the process of change (and we're talking about *any* change, not just an insight-motivated one) involves three extremely predictable stages. Knowing what these stages are – and how to effectively navigate them – can significantly increase our chances of making our post-insight world a reality. At the highest level, the three phases of any change are:

1. The Old Normal

2. The New Abnormal

3. The New Normal

The Old Normal is how things used to be before the initiation of change. It's generally the old habit or rut that we've been operating in for some time. It may not be terribly optimal…but it's familiar. And for most of us, familiar is…if not necessarily "comfortable"…at least "uncomfortable in ways that are predictable."

The final stage we're ultimately trying to get to – The New Normal – is presumably a far superior condition, otherwise we wouldn't be making the effort to try to get there. So if we could snap our fingers and instantly find ourselves happily and completely ensconced in The New Normal, we'd do it in a heartbeat. The only problem is that the journey to The New Normal tends to be more complicated than a mere finger snap; it involves crossing through the scary and unknown lands of…The New *Abnormal.*

The New Abnormal often feels like it should have a warning written across it like old maritime maps that detailed the world as far as it was known at the time – and then just wrote "Beyond here there be dragons," accompanied by drawings of very scary-looking sea monsters eating ships.

Whereas The Old Normal is familiar and well-defined (if suboptimal) – and The New Normal is envisioned as the happy place we'd really like to get to – The New Abnormal is all about discomfort. In The New Abnormal, we're just starting to try on new ways of thinking, feeling and behaving – and they seem weird and unnatural and unpredictable and awkward and difficult. Imagine very young children learning to walk. They've already pretty much mastered crawling. Walking – once they get the hang of it – will certainly be a far superior solution to the issue of locomotion (and being able to grab forbidden-but-irresistible stuff off tables and shelves and counters). But as they make the transition from crawling to walking…it's not pretty. There's a lot of stumbling and falling and scraping of knees and bonking of heads on the furniture. But walking is the key that opens the door to a vastly expanded world, so they keep at it. The same thing must go for us as we work to move towards our post-insight realities.

As you begin to adopt new ways of thinking, feeling and behaving that are in alignment with your desired post-insight reality, the temptation to slip back into the comfortable familiarity of your pre-insight reality will be significant. As you trip and fall and bonk your proverbial head as you try to get better at your post-insight ways of being in the world, it's very easy to get tired and just want to fall back into your old habits. *You must resist this urge.* Recognize the temptation to backslide for what it is – simply the discomfort of The New Abnormal phase – and keep moving forward. Call upon your circle of supporters to help encourage you to keep going. And try not to be overwhelmed by the totality of the change you're looking to make. Remember that at any given time, you're just focused on the incremental steps immediately ahead of you. To quote the irrepressible Dowager Countess of *Downton Abbey* fame: "With your permission, dear, I'll take my fences one at a time" (or, in our case, 1+1 lily pads at a time).

Whatever you do, don't give up. Insights are powerful moments of truth and clarity that have the potential to transform you – and the world around you – if you have the courage and fortitude to bring them to fruition. The journey isn't always easy – but it is almost invariably worth the effort.

So What?

An insight is only as powerful as its implementation, so the final step in the Impasse to Insight Method is translating insight into action – and, ultimately, into your new reality. Generally speaking, there will be some challenges to executing on your insight, either because the path forward isn't immediately obvious or because your change efforts are likely to be quite challenging – or both. When this is the case, there are six steps you can take to help ensure that you successfully complete the journey across the river to your post-insight reality: (1) give voice to your insight; (2) identify the insight preventers and enablers; (3) define your post-insight reality and its importance; (4) identify 1+1 lily pads; (5) rally supporters and neutralize saboteurs; and (6) rinse and repeat.

1. **Give voice to your insight:** Speak your insight aloud – first to yourself and then to one or more trusted friends/family/colleagues who can be relied on to support you and your efforts to change. Doing so makes your insight seem both more real and more possible – and begins the process of building your support crew.

2. **Identify the insight preventers and enablers:** Figure out what prevented you from seeing this truth (i.e., having this insight) before now. Use this knowledge to determine whether there are other truths hiding in adjacent spaces – and what you can do differently in the future to find other truths sooner. Similarly, determine what suddenly enabled you to have this insight at this time. This knowledge will help you understand what changes are already in motion that you can capitalize on – and how you can create similarly insight-friendly conditions in the future.

3. **Define your post-insight reality and its importance:** Before committing to trying to bring your insight to fruition, it's worth

evaluating whether or not doing so would be a net positive or a net negative for you. Compare-and-contrast your current reality with what a post-insight reality would entail, and see which option offers the better future for you. If the post-insight option is significantly better for you in ways that you find important, then it probably makes sense to try to make it happen.

4. **Identify 1+1 lily pads:** If you decide to implement your insight and it's not simply a point-and-shoot situation where the changes you'd need to make are obvious and easy, you'll need to create a plan for getting from where you are now to the post-insight reality you'd rather occupy instead. Begin by identifying the smallest meaningful step you can take to move you in the direction of your desired new reality – and a timeframe for completing that first step. Then do this for the second small step you'd need to take. Mapping out two steps at a time ensures you maintain forward momentum while also keeping your options open as you progress towards your new reality and unexpected alternatives become available to you.

5. **Rally supporters and neutralize saboteurs:** Turning your insight into reality is greatly facilitated by surrounding yourself with people who can provide both emotional and practical support – and by neutralizing the impact of people who might thwart your efforts. Be selective in your choice of supporters, focusing especially on people without an agenda and who can be as objective in their feedback and support as possible. With regard to potential saboteurs, eliminate contact where you can, and minimize it where you can't.

6. **Rinse and repeat:** Once you've completed the first step towards your post-insight reality, determine what step you want to add to the (already-determined) next step right in front of you. By doing so, you ensure that you always know what the 1+1 lily pads (i.e., steps) are ahead of you. Repeat this process of identifying steps and taking steps until you reach full implementation of your post-insight reality.

Use It or Lose It

Last but not least, bear in mind that any change – whether it's initiated in response to an insight or not – involves three predictable steps. Awareness of these steps – and knowledge of how to navigate them – is essential to successfully transforming your insight into reality. As you leave the familiar (if suboptimal) confines of The Old Normal and begin your journey toward The New Normal, remember that you must pass through the difficult and uncomfortable New Abnormal. Your resolve will be tested and you will be tempted to fall back into the familiar habits of The Old Normal. *You must resist this urge.* Your persistence will be rewarded by your ability to live your new reality – which, by your own calculation, is both superior to your current reality and worth the effort it takes to bring it to fruition.

CHAPTER 9
Conclusion

I have no memory of what happened in the three or four minutes after I spotted the shark swimming towards me. Apparently, primal fear interferes with the brain's ability to transfer experiences to long-term memory, so those moments are probably lost forever.

I was on a business trip to San Diego and had a few free hours of daylight after my meetings ended and before my plane back home the following morning. Not wanting to miss the opportunity to enjoy a beautiful afternoon in sunny California, I drove down towards the beach and searched out a dive shop. I didn't have enough time before my morning flight to properly decompress following an actual scuba dive, so I figured I'd just rent some snorkel gear and have fun splashing around in the surf just offshore. I asked the guys at the dive shop for recommendations about the best local places to snorkel, and they replied that I should, "Drive down to the beach, hang a left and drive until you see a bunch of snorkelers out in the water. You'll see the place we mean when you get there."

Armed with this insider information and my rental gear, I headed down to the beach – and, sure enough, the spot that they were talking about was immediately obvious. About a hundred yards from shore there were a handful of snorkelers floating around in the water, apparently mesmerized by whatever was out there.

Eve Grodnitzky

Eager to see what all the fuss was about, I donned my gear and waded into the ocean, shuffling out until the water was about waist-deep and then slipping the rest of the way into the water and starting to swim. The area appeared to be a massive sand bar, as it didn't seem to be getting much deeper as I swam further away from shore, and visibility wasn't great because of all the sand that was being stirred up by the waves.

Suddenly, out of the sandy water in front of me, a shape appeared, swimming directly towards me. The shape and the slithering movement were unmistakable.

Shark.

The next thing I knew, I was standing near the shore, in water that was only knee-deep, looking back out towards the group of distant snorkelers and trying not to hyperventilate. I assume I swam back to shore, but I have no memory of it. For all I know I levitated. Or perhaps I walked on water like the "Jesus Lizards" of Central and South America.

Standing there, trying to catch my breath, I continued to look out at the snorkelers, who seemed to be having a jolly good time, completely unaware that they were in mortal danger. And then suddenly, it dawned on me what they were all looking at. *They were looking at sharks.* And those sharks were, apparently, not eating them. In fact, that's actually why the guys at the dive shop had sent me here – so that I could snorkel with sharks.

Intellectually, it all made sense. Whatever type of sharks those were out there (leopard, as it turns out), they were apparently perfectly safe to swim with. So I should just wade back into the water and swim on out there right now.

Yep, that's what I should do…Any second now…No reason to keep standing here on the shore…Nothing to be afraid of…Nope, nothing at all…

And so I stood there for another twenty minutes, frozen between two intense urges. My body's primal drive for self-preservation desperately

Conclusion

trying to keep me safely on shore – versus my general curiosity and intellectual reasoning urging me to join the other snorkelers. Again and again I tried to will myself to swim back out there...but my body wouldn't move.

Then, finally, a little voice in my head said, "You know you're not going to be able to leave here without swimming back out there, so you might as well get on with it."

Click.

In that instant, I realized that I knew how this story would end. How it had to end. It ended with me gathering up the courage to swim with the sharks because I couldn't let fear dictate my decisions. And if that's how it had to end, there was no point in delaying it any further.

Instantly, I was unfrozen. I waded back into the water and swam out to join the other snorkelers – and the sharks. And it was amazing. Floating above the sharks, rising and sinking on the waves as they swam elegantly just beneath me, I had a tremendous feeling of oneness with nature. The sense that we were all – the sharks and me and all other creatures – in this thing together as denizens of Planet Earth.

Looking back on this episode over the years, that moment of insight – that I couldn't let fear make my decisions – has given me the courage to "do the thing I thought I could not do" on many, many occasions. I may never be able to remember the three or four minutes immediately after I spotted that first shark – but I will never forget the lessons that experience taught me.

If you've read this far, you're well-positioned to become an insight ninja; to begin integrating the steps of the Impasse to Insight Method into the way you live and work. You're able to recognize insights in all their infinite variety, and you understand the tremendous power they have to change the way you think, feel and behave. To fundamentally change the way you exist in and interact with the world – and how the world responds to you in turn. You know what you need to do to set the stage for insight, both in terms of what you need to encourage and what you need to discourage – in yourself, in others and in your environment. You recognize the critical importance of a powerful insight catalyst – and you know how to spark these catalysts. Once the catalyst has set things in motion, you understand how to foster the chain reaction that ultimately leads to insight. Finally – and to some degree most importantly – you understand how to transform your insights into action – and, ultimately, into meaningful changes for you, for others and for the world around you.

Speaking both from personal experience and from the experience of having listened to and analyzed hundreds of stories of insight from people from all walks of life around the world, I can say without hesitation that insights are life's great game-changers. Insights, with their combination of absolute intellectual certainty and powerful emotional charge, have the potential to inspire us to action in a way that few other experiences do. Every moment of insight – every moment when understanding and truth and conviction suddenly click into place – represents a decision point in our lives. A moment when we can no longer "un-know" the truth we have just discovered. When we're faced with the decision to try to (generally unsuccessfully) go about our lives as if nothing had happened – or embrace the fact that insight has just broken through the brick wall that had heretofore separated us from the truth and now there's no going back. There is only forward. Onward to the new reality that our insight has illuminated for us.

As daunting as the implications of our insights can sometimes be, one thing that I was struck by as I conducted my research was how virtually every insight story had a happy ending. Even the stories that began with a painful realization ended up eventually guiding the storytellers to a much better place by the time the story had played itself out. It's

Conclusion

theoretically possible that people only chose to remember the good stories – or that they only chose to share the good stories with me – but sheer chance alone would suggest that somewhere along the way I should have encountered at least a handful of insight stories that ended badly. But I didn't. Every single story of an insight that someone embraced and followed through to completion ended well, even if there were a few bumps along the way. Personally, I find this both astonishing – and incredibly empowering. Because what it means is that if we fully commit ourselves to transforming our insight into action, the new reality that we create for ourselves will – invariably – be better. And that, itself, is an incredibly powerful realization.

Bearing that in mind, all that remains now is to boldly and courageously go forth and practice what you've learned. And practice and practice and practice some more – until the process of facilitating and accelerating insights in your life and your work becomes simply your most natural way of being in the world. Until it becomes…The New Normal.

Every day presents each of us with new challenges, new problems and new decisions – and, as a result, nearly an infinite number of opportunities for insight. Armed with the knowledge, tools and techniques of the Impasse to Insight Method, I encourage you to run headlong towards these opportunities and use them to transform your own life and the lives of those around you.

REFERENCES

Chapter 1 — From Archimedes to the Anterior Cingulate Cortex: *A Brief History of Insight*

1. William H. Batchelder and Gregory E. Alexander, "Insight Problem Solving: A Critical Examination of the Possibility of Formal Theory," *The Journal of Problem Solving* 5, no. 1 (2012): 56-100.

2. Graham Wallas, *The Art of Thought* (New York: Harcourt Brace Jovanovich, 1926).

3. Janet E. Davidson, "The Suddenness of Insight," in *The Nature of Insight*, edited by Robert J. Sternberg and Janet E. Davidson (Cambridge: The MIT Press, 1995), 125-155; Janet Metcalfe, "Premonitions of insight predict impending error," *Journal of Experimental Psychology: Learning, Memory and Cognition* 12 (1986): 623-634.

4. Karl Duncker; Lynne S. Lees (translator), "On Problem Solving," *Psychological Monographs* 58, no. 5 (1945): i-113.

5. Richard E. Mayer, "The Search for Insight: Grappling with Gestalt Psychology's Unanswered Questions," in *The Nature of Insight*, edited by Robert J. Sternberg and Janet E. Davidson (Cambridge: The MIT Press, 1995), 3-32.

6. Simone Sandkühler and Joydeep Bhattacharya, "Deconstructing Insight: EEG Correlates of Insightful Problem Solving," *PLos ONE* 3, no. 1 (2008), doi: 10.1371/journal.pone.0001459.

7. Mayer, "The Search for Insight: Grappling with Gestalt Psychology's Unanswered Questions," 3-32.

8. Robert W. Weisberg, *Creativity: Genius and other myths* (New York: Freeman, 1986).

9. Karuna Subramaniam, John Kounios, Todd B. Parrish and Mark Jung-Beeman, "A Brain Mechanism for Facilitation of Insight by Positive Affect," *Journal of Cognitive Neuroscience*, 21, no. 3 (2009): 415-432, doi: 10.1162/jocn.2009.21057.

10. Ibid.

11. John Kounios and Mark Beeman, "The Aha! Moment: The Cognitive Neuroscience of Insight," *Current Directions in Psychological Science* 18, no. 4 (2009): 210-216.

12. Ibid.

13. Ibid.

14. Ibid.

15. Ibid.

16. Ibid.

17. Shen WangBing, Luo Jing, Liu Chang and Yuan Yauan, "New Advances in the neural correlates of insight: A decade in review of the insightful brain," *Chinese Science Bulletin* (2012): 1-15, doi: 10.1007/s11434-012-5565-5.

18. Ibid.

19. Ibid.

20. Edward M. Bowden, Mark Jung-Beeman, Jessica Fleck and John Kounios, "New Approaches to Demystifying Insight," *TRENDS in Cognitive Sciences* 9, no. 7 (2005): 322-328, doi:10.1016/j.tics.2005.05.012; Sébastien Hélie and Ron Sun, "Incubation, Insight, and Creative Problem Solving: A Unified Theory and a Connectionist Model," *Psychological Review* 117, no. 3 (2010): 994-1024, doi: 10.1037/a0019532.

References

21. Jiang Qiu, Hong Li, Jerwen Jou, Jia Liu, Yuejia Luo, Tingyong Feng, Zhenzhen Wu and Qinglin Zhang, "Neural correlates of the 'Aha' experiences: Evidence from an fMRI study of insight problem solving," *Cortex* 46 (2010): 397-403, doi: 10.1016/j.cortex.2009.06.006.

22. John Kounios and Mark Beeman, "The Aha! Moment: The Cognitive Neuroscience of Insight," 210-216.

Chapter 2 — Mind the Gap:
Clearly Define the Problem Statement

1. Albert Einstein and Leopold Infeld, *The evolution of physics* (New York: Simon & Schuster, 1938).

2. Colin G. DeYoung, Joseph L. Flanders and Jordan B. Peterson, "Cognitive Abilities Involved in Insight Problem Solving: An Individual Differences Model," *Creativity Research Journal* 20, no. 3 (2008): 278-290, doi: 10.1080/10400410802278719.

3. Ibid.

4. Ibid.

Chapter 3 — The Best Defense Is a Good Offense:
Proactively Identify and Remove Blockers to Insight

1. Carol Dweck, *Mindset: The New Psychology of Success* (New York: Ballantine Books, 2006).

2. Robert E. Adamson, "Functional fixedness as related to problem solving: A repetition of three experiments," *Journal of Experimental Psychology* 44 (1952): 288-291.

3. Duncker, "On Problem Solving," i-113.

4. Adapted from www.dictionary.com.

5. Ibid.

6. Ibid.

7. Ibid.

8. Subramaniam et al., "A Brain Mechanism for Facilitation of Insight by Positive Affect," 415-432.

9. Gustavo R. Grodnitzky, *Culture Trumps Everything: The Unexpected Truth about the Ways Environment Changes Biology, Psychology, and Behavior* (New York: Blooming Twig Books, in press).

10. Hélie and Sun, "Incubation, Insight, and Creative Problem Solving: A Unified Theory and a Connectionist Model," 994-1024; Stephen G. Harkins, "Mere effort as the mediator of the evaluation-performance relationship," *Journal of Personality and Social Psychology* 52 (2006): 436-455.

11. Hélie and Sun, "Incubation, Insight, and Creative Problem Solving: A Unified Theory and a Connectionist Model," 994-1024.

12. Harkins, "Mere effort as the mediator of the evaluation-performance relationship," 436-455.

13. Dweck, *Mindset: The New Psychology of Success*.

Chapter 4 — Eat, Drink and Be Merry:
Create Conditions Conducive to Insight

1. DeYoung et al., "Cognitive Abilities Involved in Insight Problem Solving: An Individual Differences Model," 278-290.

2. Ibid.

3. Evangelia G. Chrysikou, "When shoes become hammers: Goal-derived categorization training enhances problem-solving performance," *Journal of Experimental Psychology: Learning, Memory and Cognition* 32, no. 4 (2006): 935-942, doi: 10.1037/0278-7393.32.4.935; Ming-Cheng Wen, Laurie T. Butler and Wilma Koutstaal, "Improving insight and non-insight

References

problem-solving with brief interventions," *British Journal of Psychology* 104 (2012): 97-118, doi: 10.1111/j.2044-8295.2012.02107.x.

4. John Duncan, Paul Burgess and Hazel Emslie, "Fluid intelligence after frontal lobe lesions," *Neuropsychologia* 33, no. 3 (1995): 261-268, doi: 10.1016/0028-3932(94)00124-8.

5. Wen et al., "Improving insight and non-insight problem-solving with brief interventions," 97-118.

6. Subramaniam et al., "A Brain Mechanism for Facilitation of Insight by Positive Affect," 415-432.

7. Subramaniam et al., "A Brain Mechanism for Facilitation of Insight by Positive Affect," 415-432.

8. Annette Bolte, Thomas Goschke and Julius Kuhl, "Emotion and intuition: Effects of positive and negative mood on implicit judgments of semantic coherence," *Psychological Science* 14, no. 5 (2003): 416-421; Karen Gasper and Gerald L. Clore, "Attending to the big picture: Mood and global versus local processing of visual information," *Psychological Science* 13, no. 1 (2002): 34-40.

9. Ronald S. Friedman, Ayelet Fishbein, Jens Förster and Lioba Werth, "Attentional priming effects on creativity," *Creativity Research Journal* 15, nos. 2 & 3 (2003): 277-286; Kara D. Federmeier, Donald A. Kirson, Eva M. Moreno and Marta Kutas, "Effects of transient, mild mood states on semantic memory organization and use: An event-related potential investigation in humans," *Neuroscience Letters* 305, no. 3 (2001): 149-152; Alice M. Isen, Mitzi M. S. Johnson, Elizabeth Mertz and Gregory F. Robinson, "The influence of PA on the unusualness of word associations," *Journal of Personality and Social Psychology* 48, no. 6 (1985): 1413-1426.

10. Nicola Baumann and Julius Kuhl, ""Positive affect and flexibility: Overcoming the precedence of global over local processing of visual information," *Motivation and Emotion* 29, no. 2 (2005): 123-134.

11. F. Gregory Ashby, Alice M. Isen and And U. Turken, "A neuropsychological theory of positive affect and its influence on cognition," *Psychological Review* 106, no. 3 (1999): 529-550.

12. Subramaniam et al., "A Brain Mechanism for Facilitation of Insight by Positive Affect," 415-432.

13. Ibid.

14. Wen et al., "Improving insight and non-insight problem-solving with brief interventions," 97-118.

15. Mareike B. Wieth and Rose T. Zacks, "Time of day effects on problem solving: When the non-optimal is optimal," *Thinking & Reasoning* 17, no. 4 (2011): 387-401, doi: 10.1080/13546783.2011.625663; J.A. Horne and O. Östberg, "A self-assessment questionnaire to determine morningness-eveningness in human circadian rhythms," *International Journal of Chronobiology* 4, no. 2 (1976): 97-110; William J. M. Hrushesky, "Timing is everything," *The Sciences* 34, no. 4 (1994): 32-37.

16. Wieth and Zacks, "Time of day effects on problem solving: When the non-optimal is optimal," 387-401; M. J. Intons-Peterson, Paola Rocchi, Tara West, Kimberly McLellan and Amy Hackney, "Aging, optimal times, and negative priming," *Journal of Experimental Psychology: Learning, Memory and Cognition* 24, no. 2 (1998): 362-376; Cynthia P. May, "Synchrony effects in cognition: The costs and a benefit," *Psychonomic Bulletin & Review* 6, no. 1 (1999): 142-147.

17. Wieth and Zacks, "Time of day effects on problem solving: When the non-optimal is optimal," 387-401.

18. Ibid.

19. Lynn Hasher, Cindy Lustig and Rose Zacks, "Inhibitory mechanisms and the control of attention," in *Variation in Working Memory*, edited by A. R. Conway et al. (New York: Oxford University Press, 2007), 227-249; Wieth and Zacks, "Time of day effects on problem solving: When the non-optimal is optimal," 387-401.

References

20. Andrew F. Jarosz, Gregory J. H. Colflesh and Jennifer Wiley, "Uncorking the muse: Alcohol intoxication facilitates creative problem solving," *Consciousness and Cognition* 21 (2012): 487-493, doi: 10.1016/j.concog.2012.01.002.

21. Ibid.

Chapter 5 — Ignite the Catalyst:
Deliver a Shock to Your (Belief) System

1. Leon Festinger, *A Theory of Cognitive Dissonance* (Stanford: Stanford University Press, 1957).

Chapter 6 — Turn up the Heat:
Fuel the Chain Reaction that Leads to Insight

1. Hélie and Sun, "Incubation, Insight, and Creative Problem Solving: A Unified Theory and a Connectionist Model," 994-1024.

2. Wallas, *The Art of Thought.*

3. Hélie and Sun, "Incubation, Insight, and Creative Problem Solving: A Unified Theory and a Connectionist Model," 994-1024.

4. Ibid.

5. Ut Na Sio and Thomas C. Ormerod, "Does Incubation Enhance Problem Solving? A Meta-Analytic Review," *Psychological Bulletin* 135, no. 1 (2009): 94-120, doi: 10.1037/a0014212.

6. Ibid.

7. Benjamin Baird, Jonathan Smallwood, Michael D. Mrazek, Julia W. Y. Kam, Michael S. Franklin and Jonathan W. Schooler, "Inspired by Distraction: Mind Wandering Facilitates Creative Incubation," *Psychological Sciences OnlineFirst* (2012): 1-6, doi: 10.1177/0956797612446024.

8. Ut Na Sio and Thomas C. Ormerod, "Does Incubation Enhance Problem Solving? A Meta-Analytic Review," 94-120.

Chapter 7 — Was Blind but Now I See:
Experience the Moment of Insight

Many thanks to the diverse and fascinating group of people from around the world who shared with me the experiences of insight that are included in this chapter.

Chapter 8 — Use It or Lose It:
Transform Insights into Action

Many thanks to Dr. Gustavo Grodnitzky for his extremely useful contributions to this chapter.

INDEX

Eve Grodnitzky

Index

ACKNOWLEDGMENTS

Although the process of writing a book may be a largely solitary one (or at least it is for me), the process of actually publishing a book is not. I would be remiss if I did not thank the small-yet-dedicated team that has helped bring this book to fruition.

First, I'd like to thank the wonderfully generous group of people around the world who shared their personal stories of insight with me. A small selection of these stories appears in Chapter 7 ("Was Blind but Now I See: Experience the Moment of Insight"). These stories – plus all of the ones that weren't able to be included in the book – were both inspiring and educational. My qualitative analysis of these stories provided an invaluable understanding of how insight truly works "in the wild" – as opposed to "in the lab."

Thanks also go to my editor, Kent Gustavson of Blooming Twig Books, for helping to guide me through the process of transforming my manuscript into an actual book – and for tolerating and leveraging my perfectionism.

Many thanks also to Heather Neil, the supremely talented designer who created the cover for this book, for taking my rudimentary ideas and turning them into something awesome and unique.

All the wonderful frog-based illustrations in the various chapters – as well as the large "treasure map" illustration – are the work of the delightful and almost unnaturally talented Lauren Scott. I will be forever grateful that Lauren decided to pursue a career as a freelance illustrator,

Eve Grodnitzky

rather than going to work for Disney or Pixar, which I'm sure would have fought each other to the death to have her.

As always, I cherish the unconditional support of my family, all of whom believe – in the way that only a family can – that everything I do is The Best Thing Ever. Particular thanks my inner circle: Bob Meceda, Jeanne Campbell, Polly Meceda, Ann Meceda and Matt Meredith. Thank you for all your emotional and practical support, not only for this book, but for everything else I do.

Belly rubs, butt scratches and cookies ("OMG! Mom said cookies!") to Merlin and Bella, the best dogs anyone could ever ask for. Your calm and loving presence undoubtedly saved me from many a mental breakdown during the process of creating this book.

Finally, my deepest thanks go to my husband, Gustavo. Thank you for always believing in me and my ability to do anything I set my mind to. Your wisdom, perspective, love and support have made this book – and my life – infinitely better.

ABOUT THE AUTHOR

Dr. Eve Grodnitzky is a psychologist by training, and an author, executive educator and professional speaker by choice. After obtaining her Ph.D. in social psychology at the University of Michigan, she spent more than a decade working with several leading research and consulting organizations, partnering with Fortune 500 and Global 1000 organizations on issues such as leadership development, performance management, employee engagement, and the attraction and retention of high-potential employees.

For the past several years she has divided her time between delivering executive development sessions for various global clients and engaging in her own research initiatives related to the phenomenon of insight.

Dr. Grodnitzky's work with clients has taken her to virtually every corner of the world, and in the course of delivering more than 1,000 speaking engagements over the years, she has had the privilege of working with organizations in 17 countries (and counting) on six continents. She is still trying to figure out how to arrange a session in Antarctica to make it a clean sweep of all seven.

When she's not on the road working with clients, Dr. Grodnitzky lives and works in the mountains west of Denver, Colorado with her husband and her Black Lab.